The font used in this work is Garamond: size 1
size 9 for the endnotes in Book Antiqua f(
30,957 words and 084

Series of Volumes

1.
E. Betti. GTI: Prolegomena and Chapter 1 (145 pp.)

2.
E. Betti. GTI: Chapters 2 & 3 (171 pp.).

3.
E. Betti: GTI: Chapter 4 (106 pp).

4.
E. Betti: GTI: Chapter 5 (206 pp.).

5.
E. Betti: GTI: Chapters 6 (84 pp.).

6.
E. Betti: GTI: Chapter 7 (about 190 pp.).

7.
E. Betti: GTI: Chapters 8

8.
E. Betti: GTI: Chapters 9

9.
E. Betti: GTI: Chapters 10

10.
Corrections, Index of topics and Peoples (about 140 pp.)

EMILIO BETTI

GENERAL THEORY OF INTERPRETATION

5

Chapter Six: Translation
(A Transitive Reproduction)

Translated & Edited by
GIORGIO A. PINTON

CONTENTS

A Note of Giuliano Crifò   17
Introduction by the Translator   19
Chapter Six   21
Index of Names   61
Index of German Words   67
Endnotes   71

E. BETTI, *GENERAL THEORY OF INTERPRETATION*

Volume I of the Original Italian Edition

PROLEGOMENA
TO A GENERAL THEORY OF INTERPRETATION
(THE POSITION OF THE MIND/SPIRIT IN RELATION TO OBJECTIVITY)

§ 1. Real Objectivity.
§ 2. Ideal Objectivity. The proper position of the mind. Refusal of the subjectivist and relativist positions.
§ 3. Problem of the bond between conscience and the values of the spirit.
§ 4. Limitation and the perspective orientation of the conscience: consequent historical variability of the evaluations.
§ 5. The bond between conscience and values: awareness of and sensibility for the values. The process of discovery. The dialectic of subject and object in the phenomenology of the spirit.
§ 6. Spirituality at the objective level of the human communion.
§ 7 The task of the individual initiative in the actualization of values.
§ 8. The actualization of values in the process of art, knowledge, and action.
§ 9. The spontaneous recollection and the recall through the representative forms. Interpretation.

CHAPTER ONE
THE EPISTEMOLOGICAL PROBLEM OF UNDERSTANDING AS A PHASE OF THE GENERAL PROBLEM OF KNOWLEDGE

§ 1. The object of the understanding. The concept of or "what is?" the representative form.
§ 1.a. The process of understanding: its triadic character.
§ 1.b. Understanding as a psychological phenomenon.
§ 1.c. Understanding as a gnoseologic process: difference from other modes of knowing through signs. Semiotics or general theory of signs.
§ 2. Limits of the interpretive understanding due to the different objects.
§ 2.a. The difference between understanding and mental construct. Its controllability.
§ 2.b. Analogy of phenomena and confusion of concepts.
§ 2. 2.c. The necessity of objectification, as the presupposed condition for the understanding. Objectification and style. Structure and function of the symbol.
§ 2.d. The linguistic symbol, in particular.

§ 2.e. Symbol and sign.
§ 3. Possible objectifications of the human spirit and the variety of the representative forms.
§ 3.a. The mnemonic representative forms. The extended life of the objectifications of the spirit through memory.
§ 3.b. The interpretive recognition of personal memories.
§ 3.c. The contribution of different representative forms.
§ 4. Phenomenology and tradition of the representative forms.
§ 4.a. The antinomy between actuality and objectifications in the phenomenology of the spirit.
§4.b. Deterioration and disponibility of the representative forms.
§ 5. Methodology of the sciences of the spirit for the reconstruction of the historical world. Unity in the achievement of the goal and the variety of ways used to achieve it.
§ 6. The typification needed for the legitimation of representative concepts that have a heuristic-hermeneutic function. Critique of the atomistic and a-dialectic historicism.

CHAPTER TWO
THE GENERAL INTERPRETIVE PROCESS: HERMENEUTIC GNOSEOLOGY

§ 7. The first datum in the interpretive process: the living colloquy. The rapport between the speaker and the hearer.
§ 7.a. The objectivity of language in the actual speech. Problem: the connectiveness between language and the "diffuse and reasoned presentation on a specific topic" (discourse, lecture in contrast to colloquy).
§ 7.b. Origin/cause of the failed or incorrect understanding.
§ 8. Premises to the necessity of an identity of the signage process.
§ 8.a. Mathematical substitutes in the interpretive process that are in conformity with the automation of the material progress of society. The logical syntax of language as delineated by the neo-positivism.
§ 8.b. Critique of the logistic proposed by the neo-positivism and the contemporary cybernetics.
§ 8.c. Automatic substitutes created by the new media and the interpretive process. Relationships in the mass society.
§ 9. Interpreting and understanding. Action and event of the communication. Context of the discourse/lecture as a totality in itself: presuppositions for a communion of understanding between one and another spirit.
§ 9.a. The significant understanding, considered in respect to its objectivity, with a specific analysis of the predicative judgment/sentence.
§ 10. Criteria for the qualification of alternate spiritual activities which could be used as interpretive substitutes.
§ 10.a. The limits of other theoretical activities of inventive character, their difference from "understanding."
§ 10.b. Improper/erroneous identification of the under-standing with other experiences or facts of auto-conscience.
§ 10.c. Interpretation and the cognitive elaboration of some thoughts obtained through a dialectic understanding. The limits of each one.

§ 10.d. Integration and ulterior configuration of artistic and instrumental representative forms.
§ 11. The necessity of re-connection of a thought to its author. The inversion of the genetic iter is found in the hermeneutic iter.
§ 12. The process of communication: its direction and destination. Hermeneutic sociology,
§ 13. Metatheoretical preliminary dispositions needed previously to the interpretive process: interest for a definite understanding, specific attentiveness, openness, and discipline.
§ 13.a. Affective union with what must re-live and its different preparing or integrating duty according to the necessity of recognition or reproduction.
§ 14. Obstacles to the correct result of the interpretive process.

CHAPTER THREE
HERMENEUTIC METHODOLOGY

§ 15. Theoretical phases, reciprocally complementary and alternative, in the interpretive process: philological, critical, psychological, and technical.
§ 15.a. The evaluating disposition is concomitant and subsequent to the interpretation.
§ 15.b. The psychological and technical phases: rules for the hermeneutic reconstruction.
§ 16. Canons whose observance ensure the epistemological result of the interpretation. Canons relating to the object: (a) autonomy and immanence of the hermeneutic criterion.
§ 16.a. Canons relating to the object: (b) totality and coherence of the hermeneutic evaluation.
§ 17. Hermeneutic canons relating to the subject, the interpreter: (c) actuality/reality of the understanding.
§ 17.a. Hermeneutic canons relating to the interpreter: (d) adequation or conformance of the understanding: the correspondence of meanings and the hermeneutic congeniality.
§ 17.b. Hermeneutic conformance: its basis and value.
§ 18. Types of interpreters and their own personal categories. Interference between the criterion of autonomy and the criterion of the hermeneutic reality in the activities of different types of interpreters.
§ 18.a. Hermeneutic importance of the judgment of the qualification of the object to be interpreted.
§ 19. Analysis of the concept of style. Criteria of stylistic value. Meaning of the expression "objectified spirit."
§ 20. Interpretation and hermeneutic integration: possibility, opportunity, and limits of an addition of cognitive value.
§ 20.a. Various representative means: possibility of their usefulness in the hermeneutic process.

CHAPTER FOUR
TYPES OF INTERPRETATIONS
(A) THE RECOGNITIVE INTERPRETATION:
(1) PHILOLOGICAL & (2) HISTORICAL

§ 21. Different alternating prevalence in the use of the types of interpretation
§ 21.a. Classification of the interpretive types according to their function: (a) merely recognitive; (b) reproductive or representative; (c) normative.
§ 22. (**1**) Philological interpretation (in a full sense): *legere et intelligere* (to read and understand).
§ 22.a. What is a "text"? The text as the texture of speech and as the expression of thought. Decoding and critique of its being genuine.
§ 22.b. Grammatical interpretation: its parts.
§ 23. Method and criteria of the philological interpretation.
§ 23.a. Correlation of the grammatical criterion with the psychological one (psychology of the expression).
§ 23.b. *Usus loquendi* (mode of speech) and subjective ideas.
§ 24. Psychological intention and the ideal aim of the philology's methodology: the elicitation/evocation of thought.
§ 25. Deficiency and oversupply of representative content. Integration. Allegorical interpretation.
§ 25.a. Oversupply of valuable significance in the symbol. Interpretation of symbols. Problematics of second grade.
§ 26. (**2**) Interpretation of historical matters. Its different aspects. Mediate and immediate object.
§ 26.a. Differentiation of the hermeneutic criteria relating to the object. The concept of "sources" and of "the question on history."
§ 26.b. Interpretation of history: criteria for the analysis of representative sources conveyed by the tradition or preserved in memory.
§ 26.c. Criticism of the reliability, and the criterion of sources' interpretation in relation to the personality of the author.
§ 27. Interpretation of comportments that had historical value in the life of single individuals or the society. Making "the question on history." Hermeneutic criteria.
§ 28. The insufficient appreciation of historical life when done with only the psychological, practical, ethical or political categories. Auto criticism of historicism.
§ 28.a. Extra problematics presented because of the complex character of historical comportments. Excess of significance and the inquiry on the concatenations.
§ 29. Hermeneutic task to be assigned to a history of the civilization of the life of interiority and to a history of spirituality *per se*.
§ 29.a. Interest for the historical interpretation of the evolution of spirituality.
§ 29.b. Completeness and coherence of the life of the spirit in the dialectic of mythical thought.
§ 29.c. Continuity and coherence of spirituality throughout the events of its development.

CHAPTER FIVE
(3) THE TECHNICAL INTERPRETATION IN RELATION TO HISTORY

§ 30. Technical interpretation: meaning of the qualification. Reconstruction of the solutions given to the problem of configuration (morphological or constructive): *iter geneticum* and *iter hermeneuticum*.

§ 30.a. Difference between technical interpretation and the verification of functionality.

　　　a person's conduct. Recurrent problems in the historical life that are unrecognized by historicism.

§ 30.c. Connection between techniques and personal inventiveness. Formation of new artistic or literary types, communicative or instrumental.

§ 31. Technique and interior form. History of the concept of "interior form."

§ 32. Psychological-stylistic interpretation of the artistic activity in its stylistic variations.

§ 32.a. Problems of configuration as the fundamental criteria of the technical-artistic interpretation. Phenomenological constants of the artistic activity and fundamental hermeneutical criteria.

§ 32.b. Critical review of the fundamental criteria of orientation.

§ 32.c. Variety of determinative perspectives of the formation of styles and of the interpretive conceptions.

§ 32.d. Self-differentiation of the determinant perspectives of style in harmony with the differentiation of the generations.

§ 32.e. Techniques and spirituality in reciprocal actions. Interest of the interpretation for the psychology of styles.

§ 33. (**a**) Technical-artistic interpretation.

§ 33.a. Criterion of the inversion of the iter geneticum in the iter hermeneuticum. Notice on the genetic process of the work of art or poetry.

§ 33.b. Content and lyricism in the work of art. Author and contemplator.

§ 33.c. The content in the genetic process of a work of art or poetry: its importance as object of interpretation.

§ 33.d. Reciprocity between the psychological and the technical interpretation of the work of art.

§ 33.e. Duplication and falsification of a work of art. A copy and a false.

§ 33.f. Art overpowered by technique.

§ 34. (**b**)Technical interpretation of works of poetry and of the products of thought.

§ 34.a. Legitimacy and usefulness of a historical thematic and topics in the technical-literary interpretations.

§ 34.b. The thematic of the literary work as criterion of technical interpretation.

§ 34. c. Problem of style in technical-literary interpretation.

§ 34.d. Some aspects of the technical-literary interpretation: prose and poetry; literary genders. Question concerning the use of the fundamental criteria of the artistic interpretation. Peculiar nature of the literary interpretation.

§ 34.e. The genesis of literacy genders from different spiritual attitudes of the process of communication.

§ 35. (**c**) Technical-scientific interpretation. Recognition of the speculative thought: its difference from cognitive and critical elaboration. History of science.

§ 36. (**d**) Technical-juridical interpretation. Difference between the theoretical recognition of a right of historical interest and the normative interpretation of a right enforced by positive laws. Distinction between a positive right and a doctrinal codification due to contemporary jurisprudence.

§ 36.a. Legitimacy and usefulness of the juridical dogmatics in historical function in the reconstruction of the solutions given to problem of connivance according to the needs and the internal logic of the institutions.

§ 37. (**e**) Premises to the technical-sociological interpretation. Foundation and limits of a teleological evaluation of the social world. Equivocation of a criticism.

§ 37.a. Criterion of teleological rationality in the interpretation of a historical comportment.

§ 37.b. Correlations almost constant and laws obtainable in the phenomenology of the spirit.

§ 37.c. Recurrent typology in the social life. Legitimacy and usefulness of an elaboration of types.

§ 37.d. Laws of development of a spiritual totality from the aspect of communion. The interior form of spirituality within the communion as the formative law of spiritual productions

§ 37.e. Its peculiar characters.

§ 37.f. Technical-sociological interpretation: its duty is to recognize recurrent structures in the social formations and constant correlations in the solutions of morphological problem of the social life.

§ 38. (**f**) Technical-economical interpretation. Economic order, economic dogmatics, and style of economy. Necessity of totality and unity, to which the concept of style in the field of history of economy corresponds.

§ 38.a. Hermeneutic value of the concept of style as a mean to the knowledge of the unitary effect of economic structures of one specific epoch; in particular, of the modern age.

Volume II of the Oiginal Italian Edition

CHAPTER SIX
(B) REPRODUCTIVE OR REPRESENTING INTERPRETATION: (4) TRANSLATION

§ 39. Transitive reproduction.

§ 39.a. The requirement of the changed dimension in the interpretation of reproductive function.

§ 39.b. Representative integration.

§ 39.c. Methodical criteria of the various types of the reproductive interpretation.

§39.d. Antinomy between the bond of fidelity and the need of integration in the actuality of re-expression.

§ 39.e. Deviances of the reproductive interpretation. Equivocation between the linguistic form and the meaning.

§ 40. (**4**) The translating interpretation. Translation and Interpretation. Presupposition of every translation is an interpretation merely recognitive. Need of faithfulness to the text: distinction between thought and the linguistic formulation. The error of the common prejudice in favor of the literal translation.

§ 41. Criticism of the equivocation between the formula and the meaning. Rules for the translation.

§ 42. Difference of translation from free cognitive elaborations. Translation, paraphrases, comment. Translation into another idiom of the same language. Hybridism of remaking, summarizing epitomes, interpolations.

§ 43. The translation as an art: discovery of the rhythm and of the adequate style.

CHAPTER SEVEN
(5) DRAMATIC AND (6) MUSICAL REPRODUCTIVE INTERPRETATIONS

§ 44. (**5**) The dramatic interpretation. Necessity of the concrete representative individuation. Problematics of the triadic process of mediation between the text, the play, and the spectators. Different rules and perspectives about the rapport of "putting on a play" (*messa in scena*) and the dramatic text.

§ 45. Process of representative individuation. Need of unity, coordination, and synthesis of the elements of the play. Search for the spectacular key of the dramatic text.

§ 45.a. The methodical criteria of the dramatic interpretation. Duty of the director. Rapports during the directive animation.

§ 45.b. Phases of the dramatic interpretation according to the views of Gordon Craig (English, 1872-1966) and Jacques Copeau (French, 1879-1949).

§ 46. Duty and method of actors in the process of their personal representation.

§ 46.a. Again on duty and method of actors in the process of their individual representation.

§ 46.b. Methods of direction in the process of individuation: risks and needs.

§ 46.c. Criteria of the dramatic interpretation which were proposed by Constantin Stanislavski (Russian, 1863-1938).

§ 46.d. Obligations of the actors concerning the canons of hermeneutic autonomy and totality. Needs of subordination, unity, and consonance.

§ 47. Variety of interpretive conceptions manifested in the reproductive function. Variations in the auditory and visual sensitiveness.

§ 48. Relations between theatrical and cinematographical representations. Comparison between the duties of the two classes of directors.

§ 48.a. Divergences of the representations from the hermeneutic task: (A) direct tendency of placing the theatrical interpretation on the same level of the cinematographical realization.

§ 48.b. (B) Divergences due to the arbitrium conferred to the interpreter.

§ 49. (**6**) Interpretation of music. The process of individuation and integration: Technique and reproductive art of music.

§ 49.a. Presupposition to the musical performance: the recognitive interpretation of the musical text.

§ 49.b. Premises to the criteria of method of the musical interpretation.

§ 50. Search for the orchestral key of the musical text. Appreciation of the correspondence of the means to the reproductive goal.

§ 51. Interceding link between the lyric content of the soul and the technical complex of instruments for the melodic expression in the musical composition and in the musical interpretation.

§ 52. Necessity of totality and consonance between discursive thought and visual or musical image. Opera and drama. Scenery and film. Situation evoked in the script (*libretto*), as the source of inspiration.

CHAPTER EIGHT
(C) INTERPRETATION IN NORMATIVE FUNCTION
(7) GIURIDICAL INTERPRETATION

§ 53. Problem of understanding in order to decide, act, and respect precepts that must be followed. Common problematics for the juridical and theological interpretation.
§ 53.a. Dialectic link between language and thought in the normative function of the interpretation.
§ 53.b. Antinomy between the obligation of subordination and the need of initiative in the actuality of the understanding. Heterogenesis of meanings in the dogmatic orientation.
§ 54. (7) Interpretation in the life of rights. Normative function of the interpretation of a recognized right: a) interpretation and application; b) interpretation and juridical qualification; c) interpretation and dogmatic construction.
§ 55. Interceding link between historical recognition & integrative development of a norm. Necessity of maintaining the intrinsic coherence & of the juridical order in the succession of norms or in the concourse with other coexisting orders. Duty of adaptation & evolving efficiency of the juridical interpretation.
§ 56. Interpretation and integration. Interpretation and discretion.
§ 57. Auto-integration for an analogical interpretation: congruency of the *ratio iuris*. Limits and exclusion of analogy.
§ 58. Task of making people to understand; exclusion of a different understanding; authentic interpretation. Competence; object; retro-activity and its limits. Variety.
§ 58.a. Normative individuation of the juridical precept.
§ 59. Legal discipline of the juridical interpretation.
§ 60. Types of juridical interpretation according to their object.
§ 61. (A) Interpretation of the law; the meaning of the law. Critique of the dogma of the "legislative will." Normative content and *ratio iuris*. Unilaterality of the various interpretive perspectives.
§ 61.a. Logic and teleological moments in the interpretation of laws. Fundament of the comparative evaluation of the interests considered by "the system of rights" (diritto?).
§ 62. Deficiencies of the legislative discipline; criteria of integration: *analogia iuris*. Hermeneutic function of the general principles of "the system of rights." Lacuna and doubtful case.
§ 63. Interpretation of consuetudinary norms.
§ 64. (B) Interpretation of the administrative action.
§ 64.a. (C) Interpretation of the "sentence."
§ 65. (D) Interpret

ation of the *negotium* of private right. Different point of relevance for an interpretive treatment. Differential hermeneutical criteria: psychological and technical; individual and typical; recognitive and integrative.

§ 66. (E) Interpretation of the international treaty.

CHAPTER NINE
INTERPRETATION IN NORMATIVE FUNCTION:
(8) THEOLOGICAL INTERPRETATION
(9) PSYCHOLOGICAL INTERPRETATION
IN THE PRACTICAL FUNCTION.

§ 67. (8) Theological interpretation. Object: sacred texts. Qualifying the sacred text within the orbit of a church or religious confession. Interpretation: literal, allegorical, theological; sacred and profane hermeneutic. *Analogia fidei*. Tie the interpreter to a religious credo, to a theological dogmatics or to the hermeneutic criteria determined by an ecclesiastic tradition.

§ 68. Exigency of directives and limits for the interpretive competence of the faithful in regards to the repercussions of an eschatological vision on moral conscience and practical individual conduct.

§ 69. Free individual examination allowed to the faithful of the protestant religion. Controversy about the acceptability and the limits of an interpretation critical-historical of the biblical texts, interested in the separation of the
        Christian message (kerygma) from the mythical semantical entity.

§ 70. (9) Psychological interpretation in recognitive and practical function. Its character of divinatory interpretation; the diagnostic and explicative kinds.

§ 70.a. Different fields of inquiry: physiological and psych typical diagnostic; psychology of animal comportment analysed by behaviorism.

§ 71. Gnoseology of introspection and self-knowledge. Hermeneutic currents of modern psychology. Premise to the synthetic study of the sentiment or of the psychic wholeness.

§ 72. Explication of indications of (auspicious) symptoms, evaluative orientations of practical interest.

CHAPTER TEN
HERMENEUTIC PHENOMENOLOGY:
HISTORIC EVENTS AND EDUCATIONAL
FUNCTION OF INTERPRETATION

§ 73. Phenomenology of the interpretive task in its historical course.

§ 73.a. Recurring incompleteness of the epistemological result. Equivocity of meaning and variability of interpretation. Consequent involution to the isolation of concepts and to the degradation of representative instruments.

§ 74. Fluctuating existence of the interpretive conceptions. Corrosion of the operative hermeneutic instruments. Change of frame and the *duplex interpretatio*.

§ 75. Survival of works of art, thought, and action due to continuative tradition.

§ 75.a. Posthumous life and re-births. Reception, transformation, reform, development of secondary dependent attachments (*addentellati*) and new creation based on reminiscences. Productive misunderstandings.

§ 76. Growth and spiritual generation; perennial educational vocation generated by the relics of the past preserved in tradition.
§ 76.a. Self-knowledge derived from the civilization of the past historical epochs. Self-education. Humanism and historic consciousness of *humanitas*.
§ 77. Radical transcendence caused by the single individual in the communion with humanity. *Viventium ac defunctorum communio*.
§ 77.a. Education of humankind. Formation of the historical sense as the sense of continuity in the spirit of tolerance.

A NOTE OF THE CURATOR GIULIANO CRIFÒ

Emilio Betti began to write the *General Theory of Interpretation* on 17 February 1947 and, by June, the systematic partition was done. Eight years later, the work was complete. In the Preface, written on 17 February 1955, Betti was offering some essential indications about the genesis and the development of the work. In a particular way, he was clarifying the finality and the limits of the work done. He had not elaborated a complete system of hermeneutics but offered a series, as much as possible coherent, of discussions on various hermeneutic problems, which, for himself and those who preceded him, constituted specific objects of meditation. The intention was, therefore, that of presenting a useful subsidy and an impulse to the deepening of such meditations, so that the most reflective readers could draw from the discussions some extra incitements.

This work condenses an entire life of thought. The *General Theory of Interpretation* was published not only for the availability of an editor like Antonio Giuffrè, but also for the renunciation by the author of utilizing many short notes, extracts, and marginal annotations. There were also repeated corrections, amelioration, and additions, that is, conspicuous signs of the meditations that will be manifested in the writings successive to the year 1955: academic courses from "Problematics of international law" to the courses of comparative law, to the second volume of the "Institutions of Roman Right"; lessons and conferences abroad; Congress Reports; scripts related to the fundamental discussion with R. Bultmann and with H. G. Gadamer, *Wahrheit und Methode*, 1960 (which controversy was compared to that between Savigny and Thibaut); the heroic auto-translation into German of the *General Theory of Interpretation*, from 1964 to 1967, when the work was published. Betti continued to listen, learn, dig into the hermeneutic problems until the last days of his life. Hs last appearance was at Saltsburg, on June 1968, lecturing on "Hermeneutik als Weg heutiger Wissenschaft," two months before dying.

In the 1950's, the hermeneutic problematics was largely esoteric. The *General Theory of Interpretation*, a pioneer work, was destined to be considered, during the life of its author, a classic in the field, at the side of the writings of Schleiermacher and Dilthey. For long time out of print, and as a forerunner in the coming times, this work is reprinted in the first centennial of the birth of Betti, in a time of different cultural climate eminently characterized by a diffused sensibility for the hermeneutic studies. We must say that is a sensibility directly generated and widely favored by Betti's thought, paradoxically more known abroad than in Italy, and with the debt to him, which is not always acknowledge, but it is undeniable The present initiative would also like to clarify that comprehensible difficulties have necessitated a pure anastatic reproduction of the text of 1955. Nonetheless, the present printing of 1990 is to be considered a new edition, corrected and enriched. I have redacted a long Appendix, in which (beside the relevant corrections) it is gathered a quantity of additions and discussions. It was not an easy and short labor to collect the manuscript indications, at times lacunose and unreadable that have been posted in the exemplar copies of the author. Thereafter, I had to perform a control of integration according to the criteria dictated by the author for all the documents that he did not use in the preparation of the German edition of 1967. In the definitive work, therefore, in the present edition are present in their integrality all the additions wanted by Betti himself. The German edition of 1967 contains two-third of the original Italian text in the edition of 1955. I have inserted in the Appendix all the materials relative also to the parts missing in the German edition, and to those that I found up to 1968. In order to produce as much as possible a perfect completion, I redacted the index of names and re-elaborated the index of the arguments, using the cursive and the asterisk to indicate when those names and arguments appear in the Appendix. Once more. I declare my gratitude to Mrs. Gemma Betti Lombardi, passionate and vigilant custodian of the *opus* of Emilio Betti.

AN INTRODUCTION BY THE TRANSLATOR

The writing of the *General Theory of Interpretation* with its precise outline began on 17 February 1947. The meditation on the different problems faced in it goes back to a long preceding time. On 14 November 1927, at Milan, the author treated the *hermeneutica iuris* in the historical inquiry of rights (§ 36)[1]; on 18 June 1942, at the Lombard Institute explicated the hermeneutic nature (§ 40) of a translation of the phenomenology and logic of Hegel initiated in the early 1938; in a course given in 1943 and in the relative assigned readings the author reflected on the gnoseology of the axiological judgment, which successively became the theme of the present prolegomena.[2] In June 1947, he sent to Adelchi Baratono a defined systematic scheme of the theory that he was elaborating.[3] In March 1948, he redacted his contribution "erganzenden Rechtsfortbildung als Aufgabe der richterlichen Gesetzesauslegung" for the *Festschrift f. Leo Raape* (pp. 379-399); and in April, a prolusion on the civilist categories of the interpretation[4] It was like a hermeneutic manifest, translated into German as *Zur Grundlegung einer allgemeinen Auslegunslehre: ein hermeneutisches Manifest*, enriched with critical arguments on the topical contemporary literature of which the author became aware. This *Manifest* became inserted in *Festschrift f. Enrst Rabel* (vol. II, 79-168). In the academic course on Civil Right of 1948-1949, he treated of the general theory of juridical interpretation, which became published in a book on *The interpretation of the law and the juridical actions*.[5] In other occasions, he investigated single hermeneutic problems: the form and substance of the *interpretatio prudentium*, for the Congress of the History of Universal Right in Verona in September 1948;[6] the mode of the Universal Right[7]; on 3 July 1950 he composed for a conference "Jurisprudenz und Rechsgeschichte vor dem Problem der Auslegung";[8] on 4 June 1951, "Probleme der Uebersetzung und der nach-bildenden Auslegung."[9] In researches dedicated to special themes of the history of right,[10] the author had the opportunity of taking advantage of its achieved conscious level of acquisition of the hermeneutic theory. Such consciousness of his was sympathetically acknowledge in a critical recension made by Pietro De Francisci[11].

In the pages that are now published some discrepancies exist. Some stratifications and un-rescinded repetitions will reveal to the patient reader a work that was not composed with ease at a table, with abundance time at disposition, in the quietness of a private library, but in successive returns to the same script, with the anxiety produced by a thought kept alive by the hermeneutic problematics. The thought was not mine alone, it was fired at the encounter with that of familiar great thinkers, but also by the words of less known authors and by the reading of books of high interest and, over all, by peoples truly alive. For instance, the author was at Marburg for the summer courses, in 1952, 1953, 1954. The exposition of the book shows the traces, also in the succession of paragraphs and the over accumulation of one note after another, of the multiple incitements to the deepening of a problematics that came to the author from other writers or interlocutors.[12]

These pages, therefore, reflect a discussion that is far from being concluded by having exhausted its various problems and become closed. They are pages that reflect a development in contraries, in the sense that it is a re-examination and critical control of foreign views with a reasoned and enlightened adhesion.

In the discussion, we particularly utilized the content and the scientific values elaborated in the running and frame of speculative systems to which we are not necessarily tied: for example, those of N. Hartmann, E. Husserl, and W. M. Urban. Whoever, with a corrosive superficiality of judgment, will accuse us of eclecticism will certainly show of having misunderstood our assumptions. In reality our aim is the production of a general theory of interpretation that, though animated by the faith in the human spirit, wants to remain on the phenomenological ground of science (*bei den Sachen selbst*), without adopting any particular system of philosophy. The particular care given to the examination of the previous literature also obeys to the scientific exigency of the work. There where this is missing, in our opinion, there is the lack of the awareness of genial scientific systematizations like that of N. Hartmann (*Problem des geistigen Seins*), or precious and suggestive contributions like that of Rothacker on "dogmatische Denkform in den Geisteswissenschaften." We omitted not a few notes, excerpts, marginal annotations that could have been utilized, because their elaboration would have required a further deferment. In the years 1951-1952, 1952-1953, 1953-1954, we tested in the course of teaching the hermeneutic theory we constructed, with the constant intention of clarifying its problematics with the right formulation of its questions. In the academic course 1953-1954, twenty-six lessons were dedicated to the general hermeneutic theory and eleven lessons to the theory of juridical interpretation. Stronger out of such experience, the author proposed to the Faculties of Jurisprudence in Rome and Camerino, to approve a university institution as "Institute of the Theory of Interpretation."

The author humbly recognized to have not succeeded in developing a definitive system of hermeneutics.[13] He knows very well how much such task is superior to its own forces. Its precise intent was to offer a series, for as much as possible coherent, of discussions on the different hermeneutic problems that for him, and those who preceded him, have been object of meditations. The various conversations, which may seem bookish and poor of experience and original insights, may offer to the more careful readers a useful subsidy and an encouragement toward the task of deepening the reflection on the proposed problems. Certainly—as H. Kreller was observing in his review—no one would find here a pocket guide useful for the interpretive practice in the single various fields to which each one of us addresses its own interest. In times like ours that suffer the barbarous specialization—as Ortega y Gasset used to say—it may be convenient for the cultivators of the various sciences of the spirit—to pay attention to what these sciences have that is common. To possess a complete system is somewhat irrelevant: what counts is that from these discussions the readers would receive further stimulations to stick to the hermeneutic path. To this, we may apply the aphorism of Nietzsche *Menschliches* (I, 178: das Unvollständige als das Wirksame): "mitunter ist die reliefartig unvollständige Darstellung eines Gedankens wirksamer als die erschöpfende Ausführung."

In the midst of this laborious period of eight years, the author was deprived of his companion of all hours, with whom nonetheless he continued in spirit the interrupted colloquy. To dedicate to him these pages was the sacred duty and the memorial profession of faith of the one who with him walked on the common pathway.[14]

CHAPTER SIX
(B) REPRODUCTIVE INTERPRETATION
(4) TRANSLATION

§ 39. Transitive reproduction.

§ 39.a. The requirement of the changed dimension in the interpretation of reproductive function.

§ 39.b. Representative integration.

§ 39.c. Methodical criteria of the various types of the reproductive interpretation.

§ 39.d. Antinomy between the bond of fidelity and the need of integration in the actuality of re-expression.

§ 39.e. Deviances of the reproductive interpretation. Equivocation between the linguistic form and the meaning.

§ 40. (**4**) The translating interpretation. Translation and Interpretation. Presupposition of every translation is an interpretation merely recognitive. Need of faithfulness to the text: distinction between thought and the linguistic formulation. The error of the common prejudice in favor of the literal translation.

§ 41. Criticism of the equivocation between the formula and the meaning. Rules for the translation.

§ 42. Difference of translation from free cognitive elaborations. Translation, paraphrases, comment. Translation into another idiom of the same language. Hybridism of remaking, summarizing epitomes, interpolations.

§ 43. The translation as an art: discovery of the rhythm and of the adequate style.

§ 39. Transitive Reproduction Through A Change of Dimension

If in a function merely *recognitive*, the interpretation aims at an understanding of the manifestation of a thought or of a practical comportment, by considering them under the philological, historical or technical profile;—on the contrary, in a *reproductive* or *representative* function, the interpretation aims at making someone to understand the expression of thought that has been objectified in a literary, dramatic, musical opus, or the comportment, which has been translated into a drama (or dramatized). Verily, even in a merely recognitive function, the interpretation, as a spiritual fact, consists in a re-thinking that is an interior reproducing, a re-evocation from within,[15] which is a reproductive constructing and brings to recreate and actualize thoughts, conceptions, and orientations locked up or implicit in the representative form or the comportment that are to be interpreted. The historical and social reality that is given to us only in its recognizable happening, or in its effects, or as a simple product, or historical synopsis, or residuum of objectified life, cannot be understood unless transposed and retranslated in the actuality and spiritual vitality of a subject (*see GTI*, § 11); an actuality that must be analogous to the one from which it was generated.[16] Thus, whenever we consider this, a spiritual fact, there is no interpretation that is not an interior reproducing, a perennial translation from someone else's idiom and language into our own.[17] But, the interpretive process that we are now considering is characterized by the fact that the reproduction is not only interior, contemplative, and *per se* intransitive: the process is not completed with the representation to us of the meaning obtained from the text[18] (or even in presenting it to others for the reason of informing or teaching).[19] The interpretive process is to reproduce and recreate exteriorly, transitively, and socially, as it presupposes as its destinatary a visible or invisible public, to which address ourselves: it consists in a recreation that represents the sense obtained in a spiritual dimension diverse from that of the text (*see GTI*, § 22), in which thought was originally conceived or at least objectified and fixed, in a way so that it could be concretized and objectified in a new representative form (language, or scenic or sonorous realization). This new representative form, which in a wider sense can be called reproduction,—whether it is a translation in another language, or a scenic or sonorous realization of a dramatic or musical opus,—is tied to the previous representation by a de-ontological knot of subordination, whose observance is what we generally call the "*fidelity*" of the representation. The qualification of "*fidelity*," understood as the faithfulness to the tie of subordination, as it is understood as the category that characterizes every reproductive interpretation: a category, which is not perceptible and thus has no reason to impose itself as a requirement for the merely recognitive interpretation, because in this process the category is implicit and is understandable directly *per se* (here, an *infidelity* will be a misunderstanding—*see GTI*, § 7.b,—and will exclude the epistemological value itself).[20]

The observance of the subordination presupposes in the interpreter, besides a technical capacity, an ethical attitude of honesty, which identifies itself with the abnegation of oneself demanded from every interpreter (*see GTI*, § 13.c.) together with the acceptance of the responsibility for the given interpretation. The sensible [material, practical] reproduction is an exigency before which dramatics and music find themselves, by which they differentiate from the so-called figurative arts. In the figurative arts, the intuition, once objectified, has no need of a new physical realization; the objectivation itself, once it has happened, is enough for the task of stimulating the spectator to remember and re-suscitate in himself the interior process of reproduction.[21]

The text [(the score) spartito] of a musical composition furnishes only a basis of departure for the process of an intelligent penetration and re-creation destined at translating it into a sonorous actuality.[22] Between the musical score [notazioni musicali] and the annotations to which we usually apply the "interpretive" qualification, there is no more difference than the latter ones give to the executor a larger margin of choice,[23] a certain latitude for a technical appreciation, of a subordinately discretional character, about the best manner respondent to the reproductive goal. With the qualification of discretionality it is meant that such appreciation has space for freedom, a zone of choices: the act is vinculated by the musical discourse, but not to the same instruments that the composer thought about, according to what is sustained by a certain historicist artistic interpretation, rigidly subjected to the philological exigency of fidelity to the "text."[24]

An analogous technical appreciation, of a subordinately discretional category, is required also in the dramatic interpretation, especially when it is necessary to overcome the indeterminateness left in some some points in the part [role] of a personage.[25] In this field, as in the juridical one, discretionality does not mean arbitrium, but the appreciation of the most idoneous methods to reach the pre-established goal for the interpreter.[26]

The difference between the various musical annotations is a simple difference of grades and of interpretive difficulty.[27] The question, therefore, was badly presented when it was asked: Up to which point are we here dealing with pure technique? And, where would the interpretation begin? It was even worse, when it has been tried to resolve the problem of the interpretation in that of technology.[28] Really, in this case, the technical ability is only an instrument, a basis, and preparatory element of the interpretation.[29] It is an error to argument about the knot of subordination—because this tie is given in every reproductive interpretation—this is a pretended character, merely practical and technical, of the musical execution, instead than artistic and lyric.[30] Art is not merely creation of an absolute originality and of an inventive spontaneity, independent from other elements.[31] The inversion of the genetic iter in the hermeneutical iter, and with it, the research for a re-expressive, spectacular or respectively melodically-orchestral, could be completed with a mechanical automatism, because of pure technical ability, without an emotive vibration of the soul and without the illumination of an assimilating sensibility, and of a divinatory intuition, all placed at the service of a task of recognition and intelligent re-expression,[32] that is, of a cognitive and representative task, not merely "practical."

§ 39.a. The Requirement Of The Changed Dimension In The Interpretation With Reproductive Function

The characteristic feature of this type of interpretation is the transference of the attained meaning from the original "text" (*see GTI*, § 22) to a new and different dimension with the construction of a representative form, in which that text is substituted and absorbed (*see GTI*, § 21). This transference of the text in a form, which substitutes and absorbs the original one, goes beyond the requirement for a simple communication to others of the obtained intelligence: it is the kind of communication that we have in a didactic exposition or in a historiographic representation. In them, there is no validity *per se*, but they are valid as the illustration of an object, to which both, exposition or representation, refers (historical sources, remnants of the past, comportments as *res gestae* [deeds], forms of the spirituality on the objective plane of the communion as material of teaching). On the contrary, the equivalent form that becomes shaped with the reproductive interpretation is something that cannot be substituted, it is a thing that has value *per se*. Regarding this new form, the original text remains only as the term of comparison and control, and it is to its "manner" that the fidelity of the reproduction is validated.

According to this criterion it should be asked whether also the *diction* of poetical texts—texts not destined to a scenic realization, in particular the diction of lyrical poetry—should fall within the field of the reproductive interpretation. This question has been incorrectly formulated by one[33] who, beginning from a rigid antithesis between dramatics and lyrics, has hastily concluded that "the lyric is absolutely subjective and does not presuppose integrations or collaboration; it is an expression totally free and independent: thus, in it, the (reproductive) interpreter would be an intruder." In reality, the written redaction of poetical compositions, in particular the lyrical one, cannot be sufficient to itself. To persuade ourselves of this, we should reflect on the fact that the essence of poetry is not "our relying on the phonetic value of the words, chanted or spelled out, read conveniently loudly or at least read audibly, inserted in the musical phrase called the meter."[34] The use and abuse, which is made today with writing,[35] has not only induced us to identify the word written down with the word said (which is, again, an abuse, which brings us to devalue immediacy and sincerity of the discourse, for example, in the civil process),[36] but it has also educated a large stratum of the modern society to re-murmur and read auditively, so that they do without the pronunciation in a loud voice, reducing to the minimum the demanded integration. In the presence of such custom, historically conditioned, it can be said that, in practice, today we are arrived to the point of considering the *diction* not as a different dimension, but as a simple illustration of the written text, and thus we have assigned to it a function merely communicative rather than reproductive.

We may say that this conclusion, too, that the interpretive integration is reduced to the minimum in the diction, is not properly fitting except for the practical and instrumental function that language takes in the common usage, in which words serve the purpose of translating the experience in generic representations and in concepts.[37] If, however, we are interested in the accentuated semantic value that language assumes in the literary prose of an author and, even more, the phonetic value on which he posits his poetry, then no one can ignore the *growing importance of the vocal interpretation*. It has been justly pointed out[38] that the discoverer of a style is always a poet as well: a poet, whose lyrical inspiration and the ideal content flew, more or less, over the form, and never succeeded to existentialize themselves completely in it, though he [the discoverer poet] had invented that style precisely to express himself in it. "Poetry," then, signifies, in every art, the same spirituality of the content that transcends the form, even though it had leavened its style.

Instructive is, in reference to this, the confession that Reiner Maria Rilke[39] made about the genesis of the *Sonnets to Orpheus* and of the communicative value of his diction to friends. He said that the genesis of these sonnets came in the most mysterious manner from inspirations suggested and dictated to him; and that the sonnets enigmatically surfaced up to his consciousness and imposed themselves on him (das geheimste, mirselber, in ihrem Aufkommen und sich-mir-Autragen, rätselhafteste Diktat). After adding that he penetrated in small steps into the spirit of the message represented in those sonnets, he goes on speaking of their comprehensibility to others (Auffasslichkeit), and says that, after a trial made with some of his friends, he is fully capable to communicate and make people understand those poems by reading them to an audience (diese Gedichte, vorlesend, genau mitzuteilen). The profound reason of this illuminating duty of diction stands in the fact that every true discourse is essentially a colloquy, in which the speaker seems to be in the presence of an ideal interlocutor.[40] Hence, at the time when printing was not yet invented, and the pernicious abuses of printing and propaganda could not—as it happened afterward—provoke a crisis of colloquy, writing was used only between people absent from each other or for their successors. Among people, contemporary and present, the live discourse was used, because they appreciated the power of the efficacious communication done in an alive voice.[41] In the *Gospel* of Matthew (15: 18), we read "quae procedunt de ore, de corde exeunt" (what comes from the mouth, comes from the heart). In this insuppressible fact, diction preserves always its reason of being, which is its incomparable communicative duty.

To understand the peculiar character of the reproductive interpretation, both the dramatic and the musical, we must get deeper in the rapport between the manifestation of thought redacted in a text and in the audible-visual form (in motion) that, in the intention of the author, the text is destined to assume.[42] The means of annotation, of which the author has the use, would produce the translation in the dimension of space of the objectivation of thought conceived in the dimension of time and in view of a concrete *duration* (in Bergson's sense). A bar [measure] of music, a phrase of the dramatic dialogue, are not made to be read, but to be heard: they are not redacted in view of an intransitive acknowledgement (which is always possible), but in view of a transitive activity, of reproduction. Here, the annotations are not—like, for example, in a novel—a means to arrive directly to the reader, in the manner that the figure arrives to the observer [contemplator] in the figurative arts,[43] but it is an instrument of deposit and conservation,[44] that is, of permanent objectification, not consonant as such with the constructive nature of an art of duration. The interpretation in a reproductive function entails precisely to get and extract the work of art from the musical or verbal annotations in which it is crystalized, in order to restitute it to the dimension of time and develop it in the sense of duration, such as the mental language or the interior hearing of the author that wrote it, conceived it, that is, as the audible-visual form in motion. In the written text (script) of the drama, as in the scores of the sonata or symphony, the objectivation of thought, entrusted to it as a spiritual dowry, is comparable to the beautiful young lady immersed in her sleep, as the fables narrated, who is waiting for Prince Charming coming to awake her up. The Prince Charming that will publicly revive the drama or sonata or symphony, is the interpreter: the modern producer (artistic director), with the actors, or the conductor of the orchestra with its executants.

The historical path we walked on, before arriving to this figure of interpreter, has been very long: it can be said that in the matter of the reproductive interpretation, the phenomenon of division of labor, which has been going on in the various branches of the human activity, has also happened. The figure of interpreter that has been given to us in the most recent phase of the differentiating evolution of the interpretive activities, has adopted the function of mediating, not only between the author and the public, but also between the author and the executor of the work. Thus, the producer (artistic director) and the conductor come to collaborate from time to time in the various aspects of the interpretation: they would participate in reviving the genesis of the opera, in governing its interpretation according to a harmonious synthesis, and in overseeing the result of understanding in those who are listening and watching.[45] In reference to the author, it is assume that he has an affinity of temperament that is capable of warrant the full adhesion of the sensibility of the interpreter to the original inventiveness and a congenial adequacy that inclines toward the ideal cherished by Wagner, of an identification (not in mathematical terms, but dialectic and hermeneutical, in the sense, that is, that they share in a communion of feelings). In reference to the actors or executants, it is presupposed in the producer a capacity of communication and persuasion, which instills in them a constant incitement to collaborate for the unity of style of the opera.[46] In reference to the public, what is presupposed is the suitable gusto to oversee the various solutions of the expressive problems that the operation of reproduction proposes.[47] Analogous requirements are presupposed in the actors and the instrumentalists: it is a question of a small difference in grades.

To the critic, at last, is assigned, at its own turn, a function of hermeneutical evaluation, which is not merely negative—as it may seems to many critics without comprehension, who may have the technical knowledge, but lack every congenial predisposition:—their function is or should be, a function of collaboration directed to pass on to the interpreters and the public the important information on the positive and negative values, successful findings or error of the interpretation.[48] Consequently, the producer and the conductor, actors and executants, publics and critics, are all together called to hermeneutical differentiated tasks that, by integrating, could reach an ideal collaboration in the understanding, in a great communion of intelligence, the sense of the dramatic or musical poem: an intelligence, which should be, at the same time, a loving acknowledgement to the one who has left to mankind an opera of beauty and truth.

Let us, now, dissipate the equivocation that would bring us to deny the re-expressive character of the musical interpretation, by denying its affinity to the dramatic interpretation, and by accentuating its analogy with the reading and the diction of literary texts. We could observe that the representative form is given here, not by the complex of musical annotations that is the score, but by the same sounds (notes) of which the notations are the symbols, in the analogous manner than the writing is symbol of the spoken words, that is, of sounds constituting the discourse, "quod vocibus lingua figuratis significaretur" (D. 44, 7, 38). If so, then, the element that characterizes the re-expressive interpretation, which is the translation of the representative original form in a different dimension, would be missing.

We do not certainly deny the parallelism that exists between, on one side, the note, the bar [the measure], and the musical phrase and, on another side, the word and the linguistic phrase—which two sides are both audible semanthemes of a "discursus" which has a duration processed within time (the negation of semantic character to musical art is based then on an evident equivocation). We do not even deny that it is possible to find a parallelism in the function of the respective graphic representation, if we remember that the *partitura*, as well as the writing, translates the audible semanthemes in visual symbols, which, consigned to a material support, serve to fix the musical and the literary texts, and, thus, to warrant their conservation with means more stable and faithful than the one like the mnemonic image in memory that has to be transmitted through the oral tradition. It is also true that the semanthemes of both species can be fixed through a phonographic representation, and can be also conserved, but less securely, at the stage of a remembrance in the dynamism of memory. Without forcing the analogy, which finds insuperable limits in the essential difference between the two species of "languages" (for example, the subdivision of a musical period in bars has no significant function, but only rhythmic), we can admit a certain parallelism between the two kinds of semanthemes, as well as between their graphic symbols, in regard to the indicative and mnemonic function committed to them in rapport to the text. However, even willing to concede such analogy, it does not seem legitimate to argue from it that the musical interpretation is completed in the philological recognition of the text by the intelligence of whoever is capable of reading it auditively, and that it does not require by its nature a re-expression of the musical "discursus," that is, its translation in a transitive social dimension. This means that it is illegitimate for those who believe the previous statement to asked from the reading of a musical text more than what is demanded from the reading and philological recognition of a linguistic text. To argue in this way means to forget the character historically conditioned of our problematics and would make the error of abstractism. Given the actual level of the accessible notions to the cultured people of our epoch, the common level of intelligibility of the linguistic graphics is much different from the one that concerns the conventional musical graphics. Today, the written word has a known meaning to anyone who is not analphabet and can identify itself with the spoken word, that is, with the linguistic representative form, thank to its expressive virtuality, to its complete and coherent univocity (to its Bündigkeit), which has no need of appreciative integration as a communicative and social instrumentary, even for anyone capable only of reading. The diffusion of books and libraries demonstrate the communicative power of the graphics. Inversely, in the musical notations it remains manifest and indisputable the conventional character of a symbol that needs to be deciphered, whose enigma is accessible only to a few initiated. This symbol has a phonetic value that needs to be articulated and inserted in a musical "discursus"; thus, it lacks the suitable and coherent proper univocity of the written word, and demands an integration that relies in a large measure on the sensibility and on the inventiveness of the interpreter (*see GTI,* § 39): and this leave the door open to a difference of opinions and oscillations.

§ 39.b. Representative Integrations

The inevitable indeterminacy, ambiguity or lacuna, which is always found in some point or element of the original text, imposes on the interpreter an exigency of integration in the actuality of the re-expressing it in every case, when he renders the sense of that text in a different dimension. The actuality of the re-expression is characterized by the necessity of such integration—that we will call re-expressive or representative integration—marks on the kind of interpretation in the present discourse a physiognomy that clearly differentiates from the interpretation in a merely recognitive function as well as from the interpretation in a normative function. This does not mean that also in the function merely recognitive it is not imposed on the interpretation, for example historical, the need of an integration due to an incompleteness verified in the representative interpreted form: the exigency, for example, could be of reconstructing the concatenations and the connectedness, the traces of which can be recognizable in the studied historical sources. In general, an excess of meanings that are not found to be expressed in a definite and complete way are inherent in every discourse and in other representative forms; from this, too, the need is born for the interpreter of reconstructing them according to the canon of totality.[49] However, until the interpretation is merely aiming at recognizing the meaning, original and completed in itself, which has to be understood,—even the integration required by the incompleteness of the interpreted form is necessarily contained within the limits of a finality of pure recognition. It is no longer so, when the question is that of translating [transferring] that form on a different dimension, in another form that is adequate to it and equivalent according to the canon of hermeneutical *correspondence*, and therefore it is necessary to proceed beyond and penetrate more in depth with a process of individuation in the actuality of the understanding that is needed by the interpreter.[50] If someone would observe that in such a case "the document is sacred as the unique depositary of the history, the unique bridge that would join us with it, and allow us to understand it,"[51] he would say certainly something correct, but not concluding for the solution of the specific hermeneutical problem, with which we are here dealing. If someone would state—*that* the interpreter is not allowed "to make even the minimal change in the opus that he is resuscitating" no matter "how properly suitable to an ideal of beauty the change may be"; *that* the interpreter must propose to himself "a problem of patient and scrupulous reconstruction," applying his artistic intelligence "uniquely to the service of the goal, which is that of guessing, following the suggestions of the musical page, the other elements that escape the graphic notations"; *that* he must stay "faithful to the musical graphics and to his technical task," in a way "to preserve to each music its own and complacent tone, with a quiet sense of objectivity,"[52]—he will show that he is forgetting, beyond the exigency of fidelity, the exigency of re-expressive integration appeals to the spiritual totality of the interpreter and to his inventive congeniality. It is necessary that the interpreter sticks to the original sense of the opera, not "perinde ac cadaver," but with the vivid, full, and sincere conviction of its validity and coherence, illumined by his own proper inspiration and almost exaltation, which will make him vibrate at unison with the spiritual totality that is objectified in the opera. Only in this way, he will be able to become the mediator between the original sense of the opera and the new circle of readers or the assembly of listeners, spectators, or contemplators, to which he is aiming to communicate it, by transmitting it in a correspondence of senses and incitements. It has been observed,[53] that the great musical masterworks are under the law of the inventive inspiration in a measure greater than the one credibly accepted, and that, though today they have been fixed in figures of irremovable sounds and in unsubstitutable definitive forms, nonetheless, when such forms are alive and not decayed to moldy schema, they carry in themselves the traces of a genetic process, and only because emergent from this genetic process, and therefore interiorized in the hermeneutical iter, can truly be intended. Observations fully analogous to these can be made in respect to every original work of art or of thought when the problem is proposed for it of being translated in a spiritual dimension different from the one in which it is objectified; it means that this opus will be situated in equivalent representative forms that are capable of communicate its message and sense to a new circle of readers, listeners, and spectators. We should not recopy *ab extra*, counterfeit, and reproduce "by tracing" [a calco] the primitive forms in which the opus is found objectified, as if we were dealing with immobile and intangible schemas that are an end in themselves. We should, on the contrary, discover the interpretive and re-expressive "key,"[54] capable to open the meaning of the objectification, its content of art and thought, and to make it understood in a different dimension. When involved in the discovery of such a key, the interpreter must be illumined and guided by his own inspiration, and he must be conscious that in this inventive activity his education and technical preparation have only an instrumental function, and precisely, merely preparatory—even though all this can be unrecognized from an atomistic point of view, which in the genesis itself of the original work would have missed the view of the totality of the content of soul and thought, and consequently the link with the personality of the artist (*see GTI*, § 11), the germinal impulse and the lyricism of the inspiration,[55] thus, paid attention merely to the expressive material, forgetting of it its instrumental function and the intrinsic necessity in relation to that content. Certainly, the inspiration of the interpreter has a vinculated and subordinated character, and stands on a different plane from that of the germinal impulse of the opus, of its lyric or speculative inspiration.[56] It must be inspiration, even if made of congeniality and humble devotion. In this, the reproductive interpretation is clearly differentiating from the technical interpretation of the historian.[57]

§ 39.c. Methodical Criteria Of The Various Types Of Interpretation In Reproductive Function

To properly come to know what an interpretive reproduction is, we must start from Baratono's concept of the form, which means that we must always keep in mind that—"*every thing or event, every object or person, every thought or action exists or can exist uniquely in a form, static or dynamic, presentative of objects or expressive of sentiments or representative of values, but always a sensible form: with this, it is meant a unitary rapport among sensible elements that, remaining distinct from the form, become its content.*"[58] Now then, the interpretive reproduction properly consists in the substitution of one form with another equivalent form. In the reproduction, we take a form—which is incomprehensible or schematized in elementary symbols and formulations, or exanimate because deprived of its original life-force—and *substitute to it* a form that is intelligible and succeeds to communicate a corresponding message to a circle of publics that differs from the audience to which the first form was destined; or, again, we *substitute to it* a form in which the symbols and the elementary formulations are reintegrated in their full expressive and human value in a harmony of tones, rhythms, gestures, and colors; or, at last, we *substitute to it* a living form, to which the soul of the phoneme has been restituted, the phoneme of which the first form had been deprived because of the objectivation.

If the presupposition of the reproductive interpretation is always an interpretation in recognitive function of the first form, it is clear that the criteria—of the philological (grammatical and psychological) interpretation and eventually also of the technical interpretation—must be kept in mind and observed in the initial phase of the process. In the translation, it will be needed, in the first place, to reconstruct in the original discourse the thought of the author with the grammatical criterion and with the psychological one (a task, this one, that is required also in diction and in the didactic re-exposition).[59] If this thought is not only ruled by the logics of the original language generically understood, but is also governed by its own law and logics, for example, by that of the juridical argumentation, then the translator, in order to understand it fully, will have to use not only those two criteria [grammatical and psychological], but also the technical interpretation, and thus be capable of examining exhaustively those types of discourse and thought.[60] In relation to dramatic poetry, we will have to use a psychological interpretation of second degree in order to understand the reciprocal conduct of the personae. (In this initial phase, there would be no need for us to check the criteria of the historical interpretation; they in general are useful to the scopes of the historiographic representation.) As soon as the initial phase with the finality merely cognitive and intransitive is done, we move to the ulterior and principal phase—the transitive phase of the reproduction—and become aware of the exigency of other criteria that are not noticed in the merely recognitive interpretation.

(1) In the translation, in this ulterior phase, we have a problem of the expression, which the translator must make the effort of resolving by adopting a mental orientation and by placing himself in the order of ideas of the author of the original text.[61] The task is that of re-expressing the thought of the author—as it has been ascertained in the initial phase—with the most fitting words and with the discourse most idoneous to the expressive function, comparing one language with the other and being aware of the unlike spirit of the language in which the translation is made.[62] This task is not mechanical—as the current views of the so-called translation "a calco" (see *GTI*, § 41) seems to believe.[63] In this view "a calco," the knowledge that is acquired through the hermeneutical iter, philological and technical, becomes an essential part of a genetic iter whose goal is that of returning to express (re-express) the same knowledge.[64] The transitive and communicative task of the re-expressing includes, on one side, an obligation of fidelity to the thought exactly comprehended, and on another side, an obligation of integration in the actuality of the new expressive process: an integration, of which the discovery of the style and of the adequate rhythm is a part (see *GTI*, § 43), and for which the translation is characterized as an opus of reproductive art.[65]

(2) In the dramatic interpretation, considered in the initial phase (which is fulfilled abstractly with the reading of the script, renewed with rereading until the signification of the dramatic action is grasped and comprehended exactly in its whole and in its parts),—thus arriving to the transitive phase, destined to the representation, for this is when the expressive problem emerges, which has to be resolved by the producer, in its totality, and by the single actor in relation to his personage and the role that has been assigned to him.[66] For the producer, the task is that of finding the spectacular key of the dramatic text and of sharing his interpretive conception with all those who are chosen to actualize it, especially with the actors. This communication presupposes between the producer and the actors a rapport of collaboration and directive animation (and thus also between conductor and executants): it is a rapport analogous to the one that intervenes between the strategist and the subordinate commanders or between the architect and the engineer chosen to execute the project, or between the one who dictates the directives of a legislative or administrative politics (for example, economical) and the jurists who must redact the text of the law, or respectively the functionaries who must pronounce the executive dispositions. (A rapport of a diverse animation, that is, of incitement and inspiration, is that between the librettist and the musician,[67] the novelist and the scenario-writer for the film and the film director.) The duty of the director or producer is that of retrieving from the spirit of the entire drama the motives and the crucial points of the plot,[68] of finding the unitary rapport among the sensible elements of the representation,[69] and the agreement among the diverse expressive means that composes it.[70]

(3) In the musical interpretation, after the initial recognitive phase, in the subsequent transitive phase, an analogous expressive problem would present itself and it must be resolved by the conductor for the orchestral synthesis, and,

in accordance to directives from the conductor, by the single executant, for the part assigned to the instrument he plays. But about this, later on.

§ 39.d. Antinomies Between The Obligation Of Fidelity And The Need Of Integration In The Actuality Of The Re-Expressing

A common problematics to every reproductive interpretation has been detected by Pirandello when he noticed the analogy that exists among illustrators, actors, and translators in their respective duty of making others to understand the meaning of the work of art that was assigned to them.[71] Referring to the diverse problem, before which the original author finds himself with the duty of expressing and communicating his own artistic vision,—Pirandello (in a rigid dissent from Croce) affirmed that "the technique [that does it] is the identical spiritual activity that as it frees itself gradually in motions that translate themselves into a language of appearances, that is, in the free spontaneous and immediate motions of the form: from the spirit of the painter, the panorama or portrait descends to his fingers, he moves those fingers, and does not stop until the panorama or portrait is reflected on the canvas."[72] Moving ahead, from the inventive conception to its implementation, Pirandello recognizes the need of the continuity from the conception to the performance. "The inspiration of the artist is not followed by the routine work of an artisan: here the problem is to create a reality, which, like the image itself living in the spirit of the artist, would be at the same time, material and spiritual: an appearance that should be an image, but an image that has become sensitive."[73] Briefly, the technique "with the communicative means of the representation" is "only one fact [datum]" with the inventive spontaneity; and the inventive spontaneity, as an esthetic fact of intuition, cannot be the same for all the arts: "the exterior diversity in the various arts implies that the interior fact also is diverse."[74] From this premise, it becomes manifest how much difficult the duty is that the illustrator must manage when, he accepts the responsibility of "rendering visible within the borders of the design" the image expressed by the poet: "the more he is capable, then the more he sees and expresses in its own particular manner." From here, shifting, because of a certain analogy (that should be understood *cum grano salis*), to consider the dramatic interpretations, Pirandello rhetorically asks,[75] "What is the scene, if nothing else than a great alive cartoon, in action? What are the comic actors, if nothing else than illustrators, as well?" And, with some pessimism, he adds, "but illustrators, here, necessary, unfortunately." Then, a phenomenon happens that is similar to the incitements that the personages in a novel exercise on the imagination of the congenial reader: the incitements would create a stage in the imagination and the characteristic personae in the book would become alive on it, without any longer the need of a descriptive support or narration—as in the prodigy operated by the beam of the moon over the Castle of Baia, described by Heine in the *romance* "Jaufré Rudel und Melisande von Tripolis." The presupposition of the dramatic interpretation is a poem whose images would become movements in talented personae whose word is the spoken action itself connaturated as the unique possible expression.[76] "The execution must vividly emerge from the conception but only by its own virtue, by a movement not provoked industriously, but free, fostered by the image itself, which wants to liberate itself, that is, wants to become itself into reality, and to live."[77] What in the inventive conception has been for the *author* a necessity of becoming himself the same as the personage he encountered, up to the point of sensing him as he senses himself, becomes for the *actor* on the interpretive plane the need of identifying himself with the personage assigned to him up to the point of feeling him as he appeared conceived and realized by the author.[78] It is precisely in this transposition from one spirit to another that the difficulty of the interpretation is found and brings the risk of an alteration that is inherent in it and is not evitable. Then, Pirandello, again with a point of pessimism, says, "A certain given persona on the scene will say the same words of the dramatic script, but it will never be that of the poet-author, because the actor has recreated it for himself, and his is the expression even though the words are not his; his voice, his the body, and his the gestures."[79] And he adds, "It is precisely the same case than that of the translator."

In the interpretation of the actor, as in that of the translator, Pirandello sees only "diminution and damage."[80] While in the persona shaped by the poet, the useless particulars have disappeared, and everything that was imposed by the living logic of the character was reunited in a synthesis of a being less real but more true, "the actor renders more real but less true the persona created by the poet; the actor removed from the persona as much of that ideal superior truth the more he gives to it of the common material reality; and makes it even less true because he translate it in the fictitious and conventional materiality of the scene."[81] In this skepsis and criticism, we are forgetting that in the human community there is no other way of making known a personage shaped for the scene than that precisely of incarnating and realizing it on the scene, and that, if this interpretive process brings inherently the risk of an imperfect reproduction (the risk is inseparable from the subjectivity of the interpreter and from the actuality of its comprehension), nonetheless there is no sense in the attitude of considering in it, as part of its nature, a sort of contamination and degradation. If so, it would be as well right, when we take the point of view of the interpreter and look at his ideal goal, to see in it a concretization and an increase in potentiality.[82]

Analogously for Pirandello, the operation of translating "is like transplanting a tree generated by a different soil, flourished in a diverse climate, in a soil of a land that is no longer its own: in a different climate, it will lose its green and flowers" (with which we have an allusion to native words and inimitable graces). Thus, yes, "we will have transplanted the tree, but obliged it to flourish different leaves, to bloom different flowers; leaves and flowers that will shine and shake in other ways, because moved by another ideal aura: and the tree, in the best of all possibilities, will never be what it was."[83] We can concede that in every single language is revealed—as W. Humbodt would say[84]—a peculiar vision of the world, personal and different from any other; it can be conceded also, for what concerns poetry (*see GTI*, § 43) that it is proper to its language "to be based [to rely] on the phonetic value of the words, either sung or articulated or read aloud or at least read auditively, con-texted in the musical phrase of the meter."[85] This does not remove the fact that the word, of whatever language, is always appealing to the common humanity, in which all the spirits, beyond the horizon of each, feel an affinity[86] and are therefore capable of understanding each other: this is the common presupposition of every translation. To this refers the happy formulation of how translation is characterized by expert translators of works of poetry, such as U. Wilamowitz (who proposed it) and G. Pascoli (who adopted it from Wilamowitz): "What is the translating? The outside must become new; what is inside should remain the same as it is; to speak more exactly, the soul remain, the body changes; the true translation is metempsychosis."[87] This is a formula to be understood certainly "cum grano salis." Pascoli clarifies, "The problem is here not that of preserving in the ancient its soul in a new body, but of changing the soul the less as possible; the point is that of choosing for the ancient a new vest, a vest that would not make it appear different: we must observe, when translating, the same proportion that is in the text, of the thought with the form, of the inside with the outside." To the formula so corrected by Pascoli, Pirandello still thinks to be able to object,[88] making his call by referring to the teaching received from De Sanctis, saying that the formula falls into the old error of "considering the form as something of external, outside," while, his opinion is that, "if it could truly be possible to separate the artistic content from its form, the body would be thought, and the soul form": thus, it would be illusory to believe to preserve thought, mutating the form. This argument, which would confirm the known thesis of Croce about "the impossibility of the translations,"[89] manifests itself as an evident paradox. The paradox is based on an inversion of terms whose analogy must be understood with the caution imposed by the essential difference of the problem: the made inversion finds an apparent support in the constitutive unsubstitutable proper support of the form in the works of art and poetry.[90] Concerning this, see forward (*see GTI*, § 41).

§ 39.e. Deviations Of The Interpretation In Reproductive Function. Equivocation Between Formula And Sense

A series of deviations of the interpretation in reproductive function exists because of the change between its sense [meaning] and its literal formulation [explanation]. In the various fields, these deviations cause a mortification of thought and show the interpretation, not as a reconstructive synthesis of the idea, but as consistent in a mere direct technique that intends to substitute a formula with another abstractly equipollent (formula, that is, linguistic form, erroneously identified with the form in Baratono's sense). Thus:

(a) in the case of translation, there is the modern prejudice that the word in abstract closes in itself a meaning, essentially, at least, constant, and that the meaning is identified with the word, so that in order to translate nothing else must be done than to substitute mechanically the word of the original text with its "equivalent" word in the other language in which the translation is made. In this manner, the representative form also is exchanged with the simple sign, and the translation is reduced to a mechanical decipheration of the sign, as it happens in the telegraphic transmission, in the stenographic transliteration or in decoding a cyphered language. All of these are inferior forms, not so much of interpretation, but of the "automatic translation" (postulated by cybernetics), substitution of a sign with other signs that succeed more easily to be intelligible in the life of relationships. (The papyrological decipheration and transcription as well as the musical one, in general, are the fruits of a true interpretation: *see GTI*, § 22). From this, a sufficiently diffused prejudice is known that the attribution of being a faithful translation is assigned to the translation that exhausts itself in the task of decipheration of the sign recognized in the words, losing the sight of the complessive sense of the discourse: the reason for this is the fear that a more deepening of the meaning for research would bring to the risk of making the translation unfaithful. Approssimatively, it would be like for a woman to have the merit of being faithful, in so far as she has been kept imprisoned, and therefore not exposed to the seductions of infidelity. From this also derives the banal dilemma, which Croce repeated with other banalities about the translations of being either "Beautiful, but unfaithful, or Unattractive and faithful." In which alternative, one begins from the surreptitious equation between a faithful version and a literal translation: what is given as demonstrated is merely the gratuitous assertion that the fidelity of the translation consists in the literal fidelity to the original text. On the contrary, we must strongly hold that the fidelity must be to the idea, to the sense, to the thought,[91] and contemporaneously respect the spirit and the logic of the language in which we are translating. The literal translations have only an apparent fidelity, if they cannot render the thought in its transparent perspicuity. Concerning the translations recognized as "beautiful," that is, corresponding to the spirit of the language in which we translate, another dilemma is obvious: either they are faithful to the sense, and are successful, then their infidelity (in respect to the letters) is merely apparent; or if they do not grasp the sense and are unsuccessful, then more than being translations, they are free renderings (*see GTI*, § 42.e.).

Between the extreme cases, there are gradations or cases-limit. The beautiful translation may grasp the sense at least in part and have the value of a useful commentary. The general finality of widening the intellectual horizon of a circle more or less larger of readers, transferring a work from its native historical sphere to a national or cultural different sphere, may assume a great variety of attitudes and scopes: didactic-educational (of moral or religious teaching, of humanistic formation), scientific, artistic, generically cultural (of information and communication of the literary modern production).[92] In relation to each one of these scopes, there would be a variety of means of translation better suitable to each, and also of criteria of valuation relating to fidelity and beauty. A constant need is the *congeniality* of the translator with the thought to be translated, in the tendency of expressing it in the new language, in the same supposed way in which the thought of the author would have resound, if thought and discourse could have been formed from its origin in it.[93] It is only when, in the translation, a new work of art is created, that *congeniality* does not seem sufficient; what is then necessary is the perfect consonance of "fraternal genii" (like between Poe and Baudelaire, Valéry and Rilke).

(b) in the case of the dramatic representation, an analogous prejudice sufficiently diffused tends to recognize to the word alone the power of provoking the immediate perception, and thus to ignore its participation to the life of thought, which must results not from this or that word or proposition, but from their full complex.[94] According to this materialistic and atomistic view, the maximal preoccupation of the actor should be that of knowing what would be the consequence of a sound, the impression that is capable of generating, and not that of explaining and communicating the thought of the author. Hence, the experience of the physical exteriorization of action and voice [*battuta*] would be enough for the novice actor in order to know the sense and the idea.[95] The producer would have only the modest duty of placing the single exteriorizations and the *battute* in an accorded order.

(c) in the case of musical interpretation, an analogous prejudice brings to let intact every notation as it is found in the text and to reject as arbitrary any integration. This makes of the interpretation simply a technique[96] consistent uniquely in identifying the phonetic value of the written notation.

The parallelism of all these prejudices in the various fields of reproductive interpretation is *per se* amply instructive about the unity of the problematics that presents the task of the hermeneutic reproduction.

(4) THE TRANSLATING INTERPRETATION

§ 40. Translation And Interpretation. Presupposition Of Every Translation Is An Interpretation Merely Recognitive. The Need Of Fidelity To The Text: The Distinction Between Thought And Its Linguistic Formulation. Error Of The Common Prejudice In Favor Of The Literal Translation

Moving after the common given premises to the consideration of the single types of reproductive interpretation, we meet first of all the translating itself. The specific problem of translating consists in substituting an unintelligible representative form with another equivalent form that would result intelligible to an audience of readers (or listeners) different from the original groups for which the first form was intended. The task is that of replacing, that is, of absorbing and taking the place (in the sense of the German, *aufheben*) of the original form, not just by imposing another form that refers, clears, or lights up the first (this would be the scope of the commentary), or that, for purpose of encouragement, would merely incite the well disposed readers to directly challenge themselves with the original form.[97] The translation may certainly be considered useful and of reference—as it happens when by itself it is not able of providing the needed intelligence of the translated text,—but its true function is substitutive. The equivalence to the form to be substituted must be understood in antithesis to a mathematical identity, in the hermeneutical sense as of an adequation and correspondence of meanings (*see GTI*, § 17.b). The correspondence is based on the presupposition of a fundamental analogy existing between the mental structure of the destinataries of the original form and that of the destinataries of the substituting form. It is an analogy that guarantees almost always the possibility of ad equating one form to the other, and renders plausible the attempt at doing it.

These clarifications about the value of substitution and of the sense of equivalence between the one and the other representative form could also dissipate some equivocations recently born circa the problem of translating. No one dares to contest openly that the translating intermediary must have reached for its own benefit the intelligence of the original text, in order thereafter to be able to communicate or share it with the community of the new readers. It is with a manifest incoherence by part of some people[98] to challenge the affirmation that the translating presupposes an interpreting, for precisely to understand the meaning of the text under translation, given that the translation (they say) must be literal, that is, it must follow the same steps of each one word after another in the original language. How the demanded intelligence could be reached without an interpretive activity remains an enigma. To clarify the enigma, they appeal to a pretended identity that exists between translation and diction; they observe that the "literal translation demands the intelligence of the original, which is an intelligence identical to the one of the reader of a poem when this reader lost itself within the poem would not wish to exit from the poem enchantments[99] and raptness."

The pretended identity doe not exist. The task of diction is essentially different from that of the translation, even if we can suspect in diction an elementary, embryonal, trait of the representative interpretation. In diction, in fact, we do not substitute the pre-existent form, but we move at its side trying to integrate it with our voice aloud, instead than with the interior word of the silent reading. With diction we repeatedly may remember the same text, but we confer to it, additionally, a phonetic life, which is absent in the inert script. The task of the translation differentiates from that of diction. The translation is required to do much more work. The translator faces listeners and readers to which the original text is inaccessible; he cannot limit itself to offer them a kind of synopsis of the text and, stopping half on the way, from the understanding of the original text, and leave the audience of new readers to extract the meaning by themselves. If to this—that is to incite, to encourage—is what diction can do, happily satisfied with presenting the text to the auditors, far from it is, on the contrary, the translation's duty. The usage of some translators of presenting simple summarizing outlines or—to those who listen or read such foreign text, leaving them with the task of deciphering and understanding—does not prove the contrary of what we said in the previous sentence. The speakers and even, in a certain measure, the intermediary *Dolmetscher*, may limit themselves in their activity, given that their actual presence as interlocutors and the alive development of the colloquy may integrate the incomplete re-exposition of the text and can fill in the lacunae, exonerating them from what would be the duty of the interpreter. For a jurist, the difference between the duties of the diction-er and, in a certain measure also that of the *Dolmetscher*, on one side, and the task of the interpreter, from another, is somehow similar to the difference that in the field of jurisprudence or law runs between the messenger [sheriff?] and the representative [legal person, lawyer?]: the first transmits to the destinatary a declaration conceived and dictated by others; the second formulates, according to its own evaluation, though perhaps following instructions and directives of others, its declaration. Analogously the translator is called upon the duty of fashioning a new representative form and has the initiative and the responsibility of giving an interpretive valuation, all of which is not what should be expected from the diction-er. The translator must move in depth and actualization of meanings of words and the sense of the original discourse of a language with the purpose of finding a correspondence of meanings in the words and in the discourse proper in another language.

We will be aware of this interpretive process when we compare it to that that takes place in our daily life, in the conversion that we make of a thought from the personal idiom of someone else into our own; which is, after all, in a wider sense, "a translating."[100] He who listens or reads and re-reads, tries to deepen the sense of the discourse, continuing to develop, clarify, interiorize more and more what he has begun to think. Such cognitive elaboration is the condition of possibility of any and all learning. Every word assumes significance in the context in which is located and the context is always the totality of a discourse into which the thinking subject is objectified (*see GTI*, § 9), thus it is clear how—the transference from one spiritual totality to another, from an idiom to another in a field as that of language, in which there exists nothing stable or immobile—it requires a perennial translating and mutating. One can say that the translation is not only—as in a proper sense, presupposing two diverse languages—from a foreign language into our own, but that, in a certain manner and wider sense, one translates also from our own language; not just from our language of centuries past or writers that we read, but even we translate from our most recent language and the idiom of other individuals, into that we actually speak. In fact, for a natural need and impulse, we are inclined to re-express in our own language what we have grasped and understood.[101] It is necessarily correlative and inseparably conjoined with the understanding a complementary re-expressing, even in a low voice, with an interior word, because of the constant reciprocity between thinking and speaking. In addition, the re-expressing is always a translating and mutating, even when imperceptible and unconscious, depending from the spiritual diverse totality in which it is done. Here we must again refer to Humbold,[102] to the fact that, given that every objective perception is inevitably mixed with a grade of subjectivity, it happens that every human individualness affirms itself with a personal vision of the world, and this is done in higher degree in speech. In language, the word, facing the thinking spirit, converts itself in object with the addition of a shadow of personal significance and gives to language a new peculiarity. In the case of expressing statuses of the spirit or moods, the subject is perennially brought to free itself from the territory of language, because it recognizes in the word a blockage of intimate feelings that over runs and contains always something more: a hindrance that often menaces to suffocate peculiar gradations, with its nature rather material in sounds and too generic in signification.[103] The thinking spirit likes better to consider the word as an instrument and a collaborative addition, rather than to feel about it as a prisoner within its rigid and immobile schemes.

If with the reciprocity between thinking and speaking, the understanding is considered necessarily as a re-expression in a personal language, we must say, contrariwise, that even the re-expressing, as an act of spiritual activity and not an automatic echoing—(as it happens in the so-called automatic translation, dreamed by cybernetics, *see GTI*, § 8.b)—presupposes, at its own turn, the inseparable premise of an understanding. The understanding embraces the totality of the discourse, as it is framed in the situational context in which it was given. The understanding is not exhausted in the comprehension of the signification of the single words. Even if they, taken in isolation, could have been known in their lexical meaning, they would not be sufficient in assuring the intelligence of their synthesis when constituting the discourse. As it has been clearly observed,[104] the discourse contains—even in reference to the expressive value of the single elements or phrases that compose it and to the gradations of its nexuses (not perfectly reducible to grammatical rules)—an infinity or multiplicity of meanings in manner that, when the discourse would be disintegrated and broken into single elements, the meaning would not remain attached to them, nor be recognizable in them. The word reaches full expressive value, fore mostly, in virtue of the connections in which it is found. It is, thus, an illusion introduced by the mental inertia that makes the translator to believe to achieve the right "intelligentsia" of the words in the choice between possible meanings, without having become completely aware of the complexive sense of the discourse. And this demands an idoneous interpretive process.

The current intellectualistic prejudice that favors the literal translating has its root in the mentioned illusion. The literal translation—equivocating about the equivalency of the new representative form—assigns to the exegetist and translator the modest task of a *Dolmetscher*. The psychological genesis of this prejudice can be reconstructed in a manner sufficiently clear.[105] It is too natural for a man, before beginning to reflect on the essence of language, to have the idea that the diverse languages do nothing else than designate with different words the same mass of objects and concepts, which exist in full independence in reality, and that these words are aligned the one after the other according to laws that are different, but that do not possess any other major importance at the outside of an influence on the comprehension of the discourse. This idea is so natural and so that ingenuously objectivistic for freeing oneself easily from it. This idea inclines man to devaluing what in particular seems of little weight and to forget that the mass more and more growing of similar particularities arrives, however, at limiting and dominating the man who speaks, without being aware of it. Living and operating always in the middle of objects, man esteems of little value the subjectivity and arrives with difficulty at reflecting that there is a manner of conceiving that is subjective and given to us by our own nature, which mixed itself with all the objective elements that it configures and transfigures by caprice and arbitrarily, but according to intrinsic laws. Thus, the presumed object itself is discovered, in reality, fruit of a mode of conceiving, surely subjective, but nonetheless capable of assuming, for the reason of having a validity that is communicable with everybody else.[106] Consequently, the diversity of languages becomes, for the view here criticized, a pure diversity of sounds. These are sounds that the speaking individual, referring itself to things, treats as simple means to arrive to them. Now, to the followers of this opinion and view, it has been objected[107] that their view will bring them on the false road for the study of language, is an obstacle to the extension of linguistic knowledge and makes inert and infecund the cognitions acquired. Moreover, this opinion causes the misunderstanding of what is the highest duty of translating, by making it a job extraneous to the interpretive activity. It becomes a business of mechanical substitution of words, which, through a choice more or less intelligent, are pretended to be equivalent. As it appears from the mentioned psychological genesis, the view that in our field generates the current prejudice in favor of the literal translation manifests some errors concerning the terms of the substitution and the meaning of the equivalency. The term to be substituted, which obliges the translator to the need of faithfulness is not—as we already observed (*see GTI*, § 39.c)—the inert and abstract letter of the original text, but the discourse in its variety and multiplicity of its shadings. On this, it is sufficient to remember here[108] that the vision of the things and the comprehension of the discourse are determined in a manner more or less decisively by the spirit's intonation of the individual who sees and speaks. Thus, a difference in intonation would confer to the same sounds an expressive value that potentiates itself in different manners according to the spiritual condition of the speaker or writer. It is as if in every expression a certain meaning would somewhat over flow; a meaning, which does not appear manifestly in a form absolutely definitive. Whoever would believe of having grasped and captured the sense of the original discourse, limiting himself to rendering, word after word, the letters of the text in which it was pronounced or redacted, with words and phrases of which he presumes to be of an equivalent meaning—which is precisely the assumption of the so-called translation "a calco"—would be a victim of the famous illusion, of which we discussed. Truly, the sense of the discourse is not something that can be considered concluded by a magical power of the words in which it is composed,[109] and that must be liberated from some words and be placed in another group of equivalent words. The supposed equivalence between the words of a language with those of another language cannot be recognized, unless we keep in mind the different interior form that in one and the other language governs the syntax of the discourse and the formulation of the ideas.[110] It is in the interior form that a diverse vision of life and of the world is reflected. Then, the equivalence of the representative form certainly should not be conceived as equivalence between the meanings of the words used.

It seems legitimate, then, to conclude that the faithfulness of the translation cannot be an extrinsic fidelity relative to the nude letter of the text and of a kind that gives no warranty of grasping its meaning, but faithfulness intrinsic to the sense of the discourse. The equivalence between the representing forms (one substituted by the other), far from being reduced to an impossible equation between the meanings of the single words, within the field of one and the other language, would require essentially a correspondence of meanings of the discourse in one and the other of the two communions of language (*see GTI*, § 9; 17.b). The equivalence, conceived in the above way, points out also for the translator a reachable goal and together imposes a task certainly different, more difficult and demanding, than what could be an extrinsic intervention with the method "a calco or canovaccio," into which the future reader should thereafter insert life and thread a significance. True indeed is that the most coherent and perfect form reachable with a translation of this last kind is nothing else than a message and a renewed incitement to try to understand the meaning of the original discourse. Even in a successful translation, which is of the essence of every representative form, the process cannot do more than to facilitate the interpretation that the new readers must perform for themselves. Nonetheless, each one of us can very well see the advantage of the true translation in comparison with the translation-*a-calco*. The translation-*a-calco* is a pale copy that tells the reader to look at the original and it is not comprehensible without it. It is a kind of *canovaccio* (synopsis, summary, complex outline) that every reader remains free to complete, integrate, in its own way on the basis of diverse helping tools [dictionary, vocabulary, information and some knowledge of the foreign language, etc.)]. When the translator interrupts the interpretive search for the equation between the meanings of the words, the reader must take from this point the responsibility of continuing.

The situation of new readers before a translation that aimed at finding a correspondence of meanings is clearly different. Here, the interpretive office, completed by the translator, shows to the new reader the meaning in which the original discourse must be intended, without the need of consulting the actual text of the original or of having to use the various tools in order to continue the interrupted interpretive process. It is possible that the specific proposed interpretation presented by the translator would be inexact, with lacunae, or any way unsatisfactory, and this is an argument that clearly proves the difficulty and the risk of such kind of translating, but it does not demonstrate valuably that this attempt and method is illegitimate and invalid. More on this can be found below (*see GTI*, § 41).

Here, we must underline the fact that a translation intended for achieving a correspondence of the senses is always presupposing an interpretation in which the function merely recognitive is constant, but the grade of its complexity may vary according to the nature of the original text and the interest for the understanding of its meaning (*see GTI*, § 13). From the elementary grade of the philological interpretation, one could ascend to the more complex grade signed for the historical interpretation, up to the superior grade of the technical interpretation in the variety of its own types and their gradation: literary (*see GTI*, § 43), scientific, ideographic, nomothetic, and speculative. In this, we must always be aware of the exigencies of the respective technical terminology, which can even assume conventional character, but it is never to be identified with the pure and simple jargon.[111]

§ 41. Criticism Of The Equivocation Between The Formula (Jargon) And The Meaning. The Various Directions (Goals) Of The Translation

Having the error of the prejudice in favor of the literal translation been demonstrated, the critique of an equivocation between formula and sense—which identifies the thought with the jargon of the original text of scientific or speculative works, and will render illegible the direct literal translation that offers of it a kind of duplicate *a-calco*—will become easier. This is what happened, in particular, to works of thought as the *Phenomenology of the Spirit* and the *Science of Logics*, two works of Hegel and to other scientific treatises in Jurisprudence and Semiotics, because of the exuberant technical terminology adopted in them.[112] The errors that have been previously indicated in general, about the terms of the substitution and the sense of equivalence, are evident in the examples of translation listed; translations that completely ignore the difference of interior form between the original language and that into which they have been written; translations, which begin from the ingenuous objectivistic presupposition that the diverse languages differ only for their diverse words, words that designate the mass of objects and concepts, which exist in reality independently from them. If the one who translated them would have kept present the different interior form of the two languages, he would certainly not have eluded itself of the possibility of transferring in a commodious and easy manner *a-calco*, that is, with a simple mechanic substitution, the brilliant brightness of novelty that the phrases fashioned in the original text offered to the scientific or speculative inquiry, but would have tried of unearthing their meaning and value following the genius of the language into which it was translating. This reflection by itself seems to us decisive.

The supporters of the translation a-calco of the original jargon, however, have been ready to object[113] "if the terms in jargon were substituted in one manner by someone, in another manner by someone else, we could have Babel; Hegel's scholars would not understand each other, and our work would have been useless; moreover, in this badly understood liberty, or license, all the traditional values will be lost—(in the continuity of the forms of speculative thought, from the Scholastics to the Fathers of the Church, to Plato, Aristotle)— including the cultural characteristics of the epoch of Hegel." The analysis of this objection finds that at the side of an enormous ingenuousness, there is an argument that must be confuted. This ingenuousness consists in the belief that the Hegelian text could be fixed and crystallized in a translation trusted as definitive, and that could oblige all students of Hegel at the present and in the future. This would be then the interpretation of that text and will be considered valid for all times and places—and this is a thesis that the hermeneutical theory demonstrates to be absurd (even though favorable to a life of tranquility), pointing to the perennial incompleteness of the interpretive task (*see GTI*, Chapter Ten, § 73). Part of the argument has some validity where there is the reference to "the traditional values" and to the "cultural characteristics of an epoch," because they appeal to the hermeneutical canons of autonomy and totality, and do require the immanence and the coherence of the hermeneutical analysis. This constitutes the most profound part of the argument. The problem is no different from that which is proposed to the interpreter every time when the historical recognition of teachings, dogmas and bodies of doctrines is considered; in them the interpretation serves the purpose of reconstructing the development of thought in the history of ideas (*see GTI*, Prolegomena, § 18.b; § 36.a). The task is that of seeing in which measure the attitudes of thought are tied with the formulae in which they found immediate expression, when the human spirit researched through them the solution of the proposed scientific or speculative problems. Now, in the development of thought, we must distinguish a necessary from a contingent aspect, according to the more or less profound and durable influence that of it is possible to recognize in the education of the human mind, that is, in its actual patrimony of ideas (*see GTI*, § 76). A necessary aspect presents the development of thought, when it brings to fashioning concepts that are at that personal time an alive and operating element of our own mental structure, whatever could be the definition or the formulation that could be propose of them—let think of the pairs of concepts as essence and existence, necessity and contingency, content and form. A purely contingent aspect, at its turns, presents that development when it comes down to find verbal expressions in formulae that are more manageable, separate or abbreviated,[114] able to render a content of thought promptly graspable even in a diversity of formulations or definitions. These are formulae, then, which have no constitutive unreplaceable value in relation to the content.[115] In this field, we find the conventional language [technical, habitual language?] that has here its origin and development, obeying to the needs of communication: it goes from the nobler form of the technical terminology, which in time may become a necessary function of the reciprocal understanding, to less noble form of the *jargon* and of the *slogan*, which are characterized by the fact that they lack precisely the constitutive unreplaceable value in relation to the content of the thought that they are meant to signify, and nonetheless they impose themselves with a kind of magical power (*nomina* quasi *numina*, names are almost like lights), creative of obstacle and limiting the intellectual freedom of those who use them.[116]

The need of conservation by following the hermeneutical canons of autonomy and totality is legitimate for conceptual expressions that signal in a line of continuity a necessary development of thought, but it is inappropriate for the terms of a jargon, even if these terms already were used in previous doctrines [instances?]. For these terms, the task of the translator—if the translating is to show the meaning of the text, by an interpretation—is uniquely that of resolving the hermeticism of the formula in jargon, identifying the sense that it assumes in the context in which is collocated: a sense, which can take precisely some different shadings according to its context. To offer to the reader simply the *calco* of the term in jargon is to leave the reader facing an enigma, which, for the reader, deprived of the original text, will be an impossible thing to solve. This is the result of the equivocation between formula and sense of the text, with which the function of translating is tied in a knot of faithfulness: the equivocation consists in accepting the terms of jargon as the constitutive irreplaceable expression of the same thought. Similar equivocation can be found unfortunately in literal translations in bad style and gusto, which, for example, reproduce *a-calco* terms of jargon: *Ansichsein, Fürsichsein* (in Hegel); *comsign* [*sic!*, consign?], *thirdness* (in Morris); *Machtlage, Interessenlage* (in Muller-Erzb). If some of these terms, as the *comsign*,[117] can be reproduced with a constant conventional phrase, previous to a definition of its sense, other terms assume in the discourse a signification that is different according to the context in which they are:, for example, *Ansichsein* signifies now "objectivity," then "virtuality"; *Fürsichsein* now "actual explication," then "awareness";[118] *Machtlage* now a factual situation, now a power of control, etc. It is evident that a translation that does not stop at the surface and wished to respond to the genius of the language in which it is written, cannot limit itself to the *calco* of the jargon, which nothing says to new readers, but must assume the responsibility of an interpretation that would step by step render the meaning of the text. It is not a falsification of the single elements, of which the formula in jargon is constituted, in the illusion of reflecting a sense that is intrinsic, but rather of re-invent in the new language a correspondence of senses, a correspondence adequate to the totality of that formula and its content.[119] If this is, here and everywhere, the task of translating, then it appears unconcludent to recall against it, to the genesis of the terminology (for ex., to he definition of Spinoza—*per substantiam intelligo id quod in se est et per se concipitur*). The values of the traditions are preserved thanks to the continuity of the speculative thought and its problems, which are not crystalized in the *nomina quasi numina*, but by an assiduous work of interpretation. In this way, the cultural ages and characteristics of the epoch of a thinker, in whose world come not the merely forms, but ideas and problems that, previously, have troubled mind and spirit of other thinkers, would be respected. The more a product of thought is rich of the knowledge, conscious or not, about the speculative efforts that have preceded it, the more intense will be the appeal and the message that it sends to the experience and historical preparation of the one who, having to translate it into another language, is called upon its interpretation. What is here demanded from the interpreter is not the arbitrium or a discretional appreciation, but rather an appreciation connected with the sense of the text,[120] for the correspondence of senses that is better consonant with the interior form of the language into which it is translated. He who lives in the tradition of the speculative thought, hermeneutical or juridical, is the one who realizes in himself the continuity, is at the level of being able to fuse in harmonic coherence the values of the tradition with the new acquisitions, and of observing the multiple nexuses that—of which the author may be aware or not—connect the work to be translated to the thought transmitted in the tradition. Here again, in a preliminary phase, the importance of a technical-scientific interpretation in historical function manifests itself.[121]

The criterion has then be determined that the faithfulness in translating is not to be found in the faithfulness to the formula, that is the literary opus, but to the idea and the meaning of the text, and that this faithfulness cannot be actualized with an illusory identity between the new text and the original, but through an equivalence of impressions and message. It is clear then that the translator should not aim at an impossible immediate contact between the author and his own readers, but in the realization in these second readers of an impression analogous to the one received from the original discourse and experienced by the conational and contemporary individuals of the author. The translator must try to realize an encounter between the one with the others, the author and his readers, so that they will be in grade of understanding him in an exact and full manner. To achieve this outcome, the translator can—as so very well it has been intuited[122]—adopt two methods, pass through two paths: (a) leave the author where he is, and move the readers toward him; or, vice versa, (b) leave the readers in peace and move the author to meet them. By following the first way, the translator will try to supply in the reader the intelligence of the original language: the identical idea and impression that translator has gained through his knowledge of that language, he should try to communicate it to the readers, letting them take his place. By way of the second path, the translator makes the author to speak as one who would have spoken and written as a member of the same linguistic communion as that of the readers, and thus he places him not in the place of the translator, but doubtlessly within the circle of the exact conational and contemporaries of the translator. The goal of the first method is reached when we can say that the author, if he had known the language of the translator as the translator knew it, he would not have changed in any other mode the sense of his discourse, made originally in another language. The ideal or goal of the second method is instead that of showing the author, not as he would have re-written [re-translated] his own discourse, but how he would have conceived and redacted it from the beginning in the language of the translator, if he had appertained to the same community of language. This means to translate an author as the author himself would have expressed himself in the language into which the translation is made.[123] Each of the two methods excludes the other. The dilemma is logically valid: either the two separate parts (author and readers) meet at an intermediate point, which will always be that of the translator, or one of the two parts should move to the status [place] where the other part stands, and this can only be pretended from the author, given that we must exclude the hypothesis that the new readers would convert and subject themselves to acquire some skills in the language in question.[124] The specific goal that has to be reached is diverse according to the adoption of the one or the other of the two methods, and the faithfulness of the translation to the sense of the text has to be as well evaluated accordingly. The reason for this is that the sense must be rendered in a diverse manner in compliance with the representative finality.[125]

(A) The goal of providing the new readers with the impression and the message that they would have received from the reading of the opus in the original language, if by chance they knew the language, faces the problem of determining what should be the understanding of the original discourse, which should be provided by imitation to the readers ignorant of that language. As it has been acutely noticed,[126] there is an understanding that should not be provided and an understanding that cannot be provided: the first, because inadequate to the meaning of the text; the second, because superior to the normal possibilities of the translating. An understanding merely scholastic, not elevated to a synthetic vision of the totality and to a vivid intelligence of the concatenation of the discourse is, in relation to the atomism of a literal translation, surely inadequate. For those unable to elevate themselves above a scholastic understanding, the paraphrase and a free summary or reconstruction may be convenient (*see GTI*, § 42).[127] In this case, prosaic translations of poetic works are the best suitable to promote the understanding, because they do not deal with the phonetic, metric or musical value, but only with the inventive content.[128] The person, anyway, who is capable of making his own, congeniously thinking, a foreign language and its literary production, in such a way of not feeling incongruences between his own mode of thinking and the foreign one, overcomes, for such works, the possibility of translating, thanks to a selective affinity. In adapting the language to the sense of the text, we should not forget that languages are not invented and that there is no sense in making an arbitrary elaboration of them: their peculiarities are discovered or found by grades and by steps.[129] It is science and the hermeneutic art that have to move and bring us to the goal of a complete understanding. As it happens to one who reads a work in its original language, the words and nexuses of the discourse appear to him in the sudden splendor of their novelty, so it is the task of the translator to transmit this impression to his own readers. In an opposite way, otherwise, much would be lost; and, to do it, it is not easy. In order to reproduce the formative fermentation of the original language it will be often necessary to reproduce it with a different content. Also about the concatenation of the ideas, the different interior form in the two languages would impose that the articulation of the discourse be done in a manner different from that of the original.[130] The indispensable presupposition of this method, moreover, is that the language should possess such ductility to allow the avoidance of the banality of the daily tone and also to permit to guess if the discourse was developed in full and free spontaneity, or forced to resemble an exotic model. To absolve the task with gusto and measure, without prejudice on the opus or the language, is an enterprise that demands modesty and abnegation (*see GTI*, § 13). The effort at maintaining the tone of the language exotic exposes the translator to the danger of not being understood for not having respected the right line, the appreciation of which is conditioned by our subjectivity.[131]

(B) The contrary direction is that of presenting the literary opus to the new readers as if the author would have conceived and composed it from the beginning in their language. The first canon then to respect is that of avoiding all not allowed deviations to any work of the same kind that has been originally written in the language in which one is translating[132]. This obligation can be expressed with the formula that the author must be required to speak in the same way in which we interpreters must suppose that he will have expressed himself if speaking in our language. This supposition is the more legitimate when the phase in which the author's language develops is similar to the one to be found in our language. The individuals, however, who are convinced that to think and to speak are only one and the same spiritual energy (*see GTI*, § 9),[133] will not succeed in eradicating and separating a thinking subject from his native language nor preserving as identical and unchanged in two different languages his discourse and order of ideas. To succeed in such radical *tabula rasa*, it would be necessary to remove from the original discourse everything that in it is due to the influence that the author absorbed for having spoken and heard to speak in his mother-tongue, and correlatively reattach to the in-process-translation the influence that he would have absorbers in his mode of conceiving and intuiting, if he would have heard to speak the other language, up to the point of being capable of thinking and writing in it.[134] Without considering the not so rare case of those who can from the beginning think and compose in a language different from their native one, obeying to an expressive need for which the native language seems less adequate, it is clear that reasonably we cannot propose to ourselves to make *tabula rasa* of the unresolvable knot that ties knowledge and the representative faculty to the language in which we have been educated: truly, it is an intrinsic bond that normally cannot be substituted with the bond with another language. The frequent habit in professional life of writing in a different language—in which thoughts are not genuinely coming from the profound root of the personal language—nor the habit of the scientists of speaking comfortably and effortlessly a diverse language in the treatment of a topic constitute a contrary demonstration, because for them it happens solely for the fact that they feel fully in charge of the topic treated and familiar with the particular technical terminology.[135]

A decisive argument, however, against the legitimacy of what we have above discussed and of the way of this direction or method,[136] can be made only if the fact—that it is not normal to write in a foreign language—is correctly understood. The criterion of shaping the translation in accordance with the attitudes of the thought that the author should have assumed if he would have expressed it in the language into which one is translating, does not point to a psychological identification with the author—which should be impossible—but only to a normative instance of adequacy that answers to the need of determining as the point of origin and reference the thinking subject, whose discourse and order of ideas we must represent in another language according to the genuine spirit that shapes it. This exigency warrants, in a certain way, the authenticity of the thought through the author.[137] If the translating serves to satisfy the interest to know and the need of knowledge of a certain circle of readers who have not learned the language, but prefer foreign works, then the fabrication of a psychological identification, manifestly anti-historical, is superfluous.[138]

We know that every language contains in itself a system of ideation and an organic complex of concepts, which—by tying with each other, interfering and integrating themselves in the same communion of language—form a dialectic totality articulated in itself, whose single elements never find an exact congruence in the analogous elements of the conceptual complex of other languages, given the peculiarity of light, color, and shading that derive from the whole. We can admit that from this a danger originates. If the translator, instead of trying to bend his language toward the original language in order to guess its ideation, tries to make the author to speak as if from the beginning he had formulated the discourse in the other language [that of the translator?], would risk to stumble over the lack of affinity between the elements of the two languages and must modify the discourse in agreement with the different ideation [that he, the translator, has] of his language. The fear[139] that such process would open the way to arbitrium is exaggerated but, in reality, is no greater than in other areas of the reproductive interpretation. Here, as in other areas, the question is not about arbitrium or the full discretionality of the translator, but of an appreciation related to the sense of the text rightly interpreted: an appreciation of the better idoneous means of expression for the actualization of a correspondence of senses between the original text and its translation. Here as elsewhere, the guarantee of preserving a connection with the thought of the author is found—excluding any fabrication of a psychological identification with the author—in the common mental structure that is given by the fundamental identity of the human nature.[140] With this, we return to the same reason that makes possible a communality of objectifications of thought. As for the assumption of dissolution of the interior form of the original language into that of the other language that would bring to a reproduction that would not be truly appreciated except by anyone who already possesses from other sources an immediate knowledge of the foreign author, for the ultimate scope of placing into light its spirit, would be a valid objection only against the imagination of the possibility of identification with the author, and not against the need of actuality and adequacy of the understanding (*see GTI*, § 17), which must be satisfied by means of the translation and by any reproductive interpretation.[141]

§ 42. Difference Between Translation And Free Cognitive Elaborations: Paraphrases, Comments, Versions In Other Idioms, Hybridism Of The Remaking, Summarizing Epitomes, And Interpolations

The translating is intended to create a new representative form that is destined as a discourse to substitute the discourse or original text according to the method of correspondence of meanings. Consequently it is easy to intuit the difference that runs between the translation and the other elaborations that, though having with it the common premise given by the previous interpretation of a discourse (text) and the goal of procuring its knowledge, they do not possess the function of substituting it, but of illustrating its sense alone or recalling it.

(a) *Paraphrases.* The paraphrases tend to overcome the peculiarity of the original language with the consequent result of a defect of congruence between the two languages, through a mechanical progression. A paraphrase tends to reach the value that words possess in the original language by adding restrictive or extensive specifications, as if they were merely mathematical symbols (*see GTI*, § 8.b). In that way, the paraphraser will renounce to give the impression of a spoken discourse that respects the spirit and the interior form of both languages. Let say that he is happy just to up held a ladder to the height of the text in order to make its sense more accessible. Everybody can notice that a live discourse could not spring up from its origin in such a manner from the spirit of a thinking subject.[142] The paraphrase is thus a manipulation, which makes violence to the interior form of both languages and kills without remedy the alive discourse, filling its place with an artifact, similar, in this view, to the result of an automatic translation operated by the so-called *speaking machines*, to which the newest scientific materialism gave the pompous qualification of *electronic brains* (*see GTI*, § 8.b).

(b) *Versions*. The version of someone's discourse into an individual idiom within the same language, of which we need in ordinary life, even without being aware of it, is due to an unconscious pressure of assimilating and re-expressing the thought and the order of ideas of others. The translation and the version are two activities that are strictly similar from origin and that reciprocally clarify each other (*see GTI*, § 40). In addition, it is of interest to realize that in the version we have in prevalence our subjectivity as the interpreters, pressured as we are to assimilate and take position, and understand the discourse of others not so much in its original significance but as in the significance that we assign to it.[143] It is from here that the repeated and inevitable misunderstandings originated (*see GTI*, § 7.b), which characterized the oral discussion as it becomes more vivacious and heated. On the contrary, the subjectivity in the translation is tied with the knot of faithfulness and of a rigorous subordination to the sense of the discourse, which we must assimilate not for us but put it in the right light and make it understood by others.

(c) *Comments*. The translation is controlled by the prevalence of the interpretive process, of which the comments are only the preliminary phase. The comment has been defined in the tradition as "expositio, verborum iuncturam non considerans, sed sensum" (an exposition that does not consider the connection of the words, but the sense alone). In the comment then the interest is that of understanding the sense of the original text, but, in addition, of deepening the achieved intelligence of it for a didactic purpose, bringing it to ulterior developments through a cognitive elaboration that can direct largely to overpass the proper borders of the interpretation in the merely recognitive function. The characteristic of the comment is the cognitive elaboration, which takes the importance of a discussion and, so to say, of a colloquy between the commentator and the text, from which he starts his moves and to which he constantly returns for verification and for obtaining renewed incitements. The interest that causes this ideal colloquy is not purely hermeneutical but excites the promotion of a selective development of thought that can be—theoretical, didactic, or speculative (as in comments to works of poetry or science)—or practical, in a wide sense, or normative (as in comments to juridical texts or theological). We may here refer to what has been said about a cognitive elaboration (*see GTI*, § 10.c), through a dialectic intelligence, when we distinguished it from the interpretation. The dialectic analysis and the critical control originate from a position assigned by the thought of the author and the sense of the text: In their initial phase, therefore, they have the character of an interpretive process. Soon, however, they move beyond the sphere of competence of a pure interpretation, which is characterized by the knot of faithfulness and subordination to the text, in order to isolate the text from its native spiritual totality, and to develop its sense according to preferential motives and judgements of value: motives and judgments that obey theoretical or practical exigencies that are dictated by the progressive movement of life and thought. Though the speculative and normative explications that the comment promotes are often labeled as "interpretation" or "explanation" (Deutung) (*see GTI*, § 2.a; 10.c.),[144] the difference is certainly indisputable between the controllable recognition of a pre-existent, concluded in itself, new sense—and the free attribution of a new sense obtained from the previous by way of an interpretive conversion (Umdeutung) or a misunderstanding, perhaps even conscious (*see GTI*, § 75). We do not mean to express a negative evaluation of the "comment," but only to consolidate the conceptual distinction that the author of the comments is inclined to disadknowledge because of the tendency of the commentators of searching for and finding connections between texts and supports—from the spiritual patrimony of tradition—for the developments that they introduce.[145] The increment of jurisprudence, after all, and of theology and other disciplines of the spirit and of the scientific and speculative progress—is exactly due to the cognitive elaboration by way of comments mostly, and not only in the medieval stage (*see GTI*, § 36.a) (for ex.: the great commentators of the Justinian Statutes, or of the works of Aristotle and Plato).[146]

Differentiating from others objectifications of the spirit, the texts into which thought is objectified send out a message whose understanding requires in a larger grade the effort of finding and understanding it (*see GTI*, § 13). For this reason, the text is the element of interpretation that is mostly exposed to deformation and misunderstanding. For a contrast, it is enough to think of works of art of the visual representation: no matter how sensible could be the happened variety of mutations in the manner of looking and seeing them, nonetheless it is undeniable that each single work has a consistency that makes of it a wholeness in itself doted on a univocal sense, relatively separable from the author and from the ambiance of its origin and from other coeval and affined works.[147] It is not so for the discourse and the order of idea constitutive of a work of thought. The discourse and the order of ideas are not rightly intelligible in their genuine sense at the outside of their spiritual totality, from which they originated. They rely on the honest involvement of the interpreter to respect and preserve their genetic nexus. Consequently, they are vulnerable, in a different manner, for the danger to which they are exposed—of being disanchored from their original totality and annexed to a different totality in such a mode of giving a diverse sense. The discourse and the order of ideas resent, then,—beside a dissociation and mutation of perspective that can be imposed on them, consciously or not—the arbitrium of those who receive their message. In fact, the arbirtium can be dominated by conflicting interests with the intention and aspiration of reaching back to the genuine sense and of giving of it a faithful reconstruction.[148]

(d) The particular vulnerability helps to comprehend in their hybrid characters other phenomena as the summarizing or anthological *epitomes*, the remaking and re-editing, and the interpolations of traditional or transmitted texts. These are all elaborations that initiate with an interpretive process and end with the re-expression of the thought in a new text, but, by the fact of being free from the obligation of faithfulness as in the translation, they aim at an abbreviated redaction, modified or integrated, and present a deformation or a conscious alteration of the original sense. They all intend to utilize a pre-existent text as thread of their thought, but with the purpose of presenting it to a new circle of auditors and readers, with the modifications required by new needs. The epitomes aim at simplifying, by means of summaries or choice of parts, to render the text more accessible. For works of thought, this process would be arbitrary and prejudicial because disassociating an order of ideas from its system, and in particular the concept or the principle from the problem of which they constituted the solution causes a fixed exterior scheme, separated from the coherent concatenations of the judgements that justified its reasonableness (*see GTI*, § 35).[149] Thus the discourse becomes superficial and extrinsic, the concepts empty, and degraded to mere conventional schemes.[150]

(e) *Recomposition, Remaking.* The remaking intends to adapt the pre-existent thematic of ideas to new fashions of taste and dominant conceptions in the ambient, or to the technique of the diverse expressive dimension, to which the re-incarnated work of thought is destined. This, too, is a deformation, connected also to the danger of a trivialization, to which the objectivation of thought tied to the format of words is subjected (literary form in wider sense). The existent antithesis between such objectifications and the works of art of visual representation can still be instructive here, in order to grasp with all evidence the different structure of the knot that ties the objectivation, on one side, to thought, and on another side, to the material support that makes it perceptively and contemplable outside time (*see GTI*, § 3).[151] The nexus that ties the value of art to the objectivation and that of the objectivation to its material support is certainly more strict and univocal than the nexus of thought with the literary form that makes its re-evocation possible. Though exposed to the variation of gusto and the manner of looking and intuiting, the image has in itself its own concreteness, and so to say,[152] incorporate in itself the esthetic value of the work of art centered in it. On the contrary, the concept, the intuition, or the principle, even if expressed in a teaching or in a dogma, remain in themselves abbreviated formulae, which never receive a full significative pregnancy unless framed in the totality of a vision of the whole or of the discourse of which are part (*see GTI*, § 9), and they are senseless unless placed in the light of a spiritual attitude and of evaluative presuppositions that cannot be capture in any formula.[153] The linguistic symbol does not possess the complete, indissoluble, and demanding character in its intrinsic coherence, in its *Bundigkeit*, which characterizes the visual image. This essential difference explains the phenomenon of remaking/reconstructing. Remakes and reconstructions are the re-elaborations to which the works knitted in the literary form—in the intent of re-expressing their thought according to an exigency of adaptation—are subjected. They must adapt in content, which must conform to the fashion of tastes and conceptions; in form, whenever the form must correspond to the expressive dimensions into which it is translated. There is an exigency of consonance between discursive thought (for ex., of a novel or a libretto) and a visual or musical image into which this thought has to be re-incarnated in a cinematographic or theatric reproduction (*see GTI*, § 52).

Evidently no reason exists here to obey to a hermeneutical nexus of a strict subordination, which characterizes the translation, but only to have an esthetic nexus that imposes on the adapter the duty of safeguarding—with the innovations to be introduced in obsequy to the technique of the mutated dimension—the sense and the poetic content of the pre-existent text. It is understandable that one translating into dimensions different from those of the original work, must introduced the suitable adaptations,[154] as well, because every expressive dimension has its particular technique.

(f) *Interpolations*. When the pre-existent plot of thought can be adapted to the changed conceptions of the ambient in which it must be used and utilized as an instrument of the civil life (Geräte *des Lebens*—Freyer would say), without the need of being remade or redone from the basis, then it would be sufficient to introduce in the text, for this scope, the alterations that take the name of "interpolations."[155] Interpolations are, thus, alternated insertion in the text and also additions, substitutions, omissions of words and phrases, which lean towards making the sense of the transmitted text in harmony with the mutated or different conceptions, to which it must respond. The conscious finality of adaptation distinguishes the interpolations from accidental corruptions of the text due to the vicissitudes of transmission or from errors of transcription caused by the work of the amanuenses. The interpolation differs also from the annotations—in origin, interlinear or marginal—having character of *glossema*, because intended only for the clarification of the sense of the discourse, and not for modifying or innovating. The diagnosis of *glossema*, in its specific case, or of interpolation may be difficult because of the possibility, from one side, of the existence of innovative misunderstandings in contrast with the intention merely interpretive possessed by the annotator of the text and, from another side, vice versa, of interpolations of a character merely scholastic and doctrinal, executed, in place of commissions of legislative reform, by students who intended to harmonize the terminology and the dogmatic of the transmitted text with the problematics of the actual and active norms and views; these students will be inclined to suppress everything in the text that result abrogated or out of use and antiquated.[156] It is necessary to recall (*see GTI*, § 20) that—even when the text is preserved immutated in its literary structure—nonetheless, in the historical transfer from its native "humus" to a cultural ambience essentially different, receives, in the use that is been done of it, an ulterior (duplex) *interpretatio*, which is required by the making it in accordance with a spiritual totality that differs from its originary one (*see GTI*, § 55). There where the case is the rethinking connected with the use of the text as an instrument of the civil living and has been translated into interpolations that have modified its primitive sense, there the text will present discrepancies and stratifications that denounce, in dissonance or deficiency of formulations, the superposition of successive attitudes of thought. This is a phenomenon of superposition and stratification, which is well known to the philological critique and hermeneutics (*see GTI*, § 23), but that acquires particular importance concerning legislative texts, the formation or historical vicissitude of which it is the product of a collective and successive cooperation.[157]

The phenomenon of stratification—in the vicissitude suffered by the texts of the classic Roman Diritto which were composed in a manner of mosaic in the *Corpus Juris Civilis* of Justinian with the intention of obtaining an active codex of Diritto—is of a special historical interest. Today it is accepted that the texts of the classic jurists have not been profoundly modified by the Justinianeous compilators as the modern critical inquiry, in the first time, was inclined to believe. The reason is that there is the wide possibility of an interpretive conversion by way of the *duplex interpretatio* that the texts were offering.[158] In addition, these texts did not come in the hands of the compilers unaltered or immutated, but already enriched with the current mutated status of the Diritto by way of post-classical glossema, interpolations, reductions, and paraphrases through which from the time past or of before they had been already penetrated by a new problematics and dogmatic, more or less variated from the classical conceptions.[159] It is probable that the factors determining the adaptation and the new redaction of the classical texts were not only extrinsic nor had been influential only once and then leaving them immutated—as it was supposed that it happened[160] with the substitution of the papyri roll with the book around 300 A.C.—but had an intrinsic and continuous character. The adaptation of the transmitted texts must have had the aim of plying the conceptions and the solutions in a manner to make them respondent to the new needs of the concrete application and to the diverse Hellenic-Oriental conceptions, which by the time of Constantine had penetrated in the official Diritto of the Empire,[161] and to adequate them to the lower intellectual level of the practical jurisprudence that had the task of applying them.[162] At the light of this uninterrupted historical continuity, the interpolations introduced in the classical texts by the Justinian compilers appear not only reduced in entity and number, but especially no longer isolated, but rather inserted in a grandiose process of interpretive conversion (Umdeutung), which began much time before the compilation of the Corpus Juris,[163] since the beginning of the post-classic period and, in a sporadic manner, since late classic period.[164] This process does not always need to translate itself into a conscious alteration of the texts and will continue unstoppably in the Justinianeous texts in the tradition of the Common Diritto until the modern time of pandectisticism.[165] The motives of the previous interpolations and of those operated by the Justinian compilers must be research in some exigencies of adaptation, theoretical as well as practical, which imposed the strategy of placing the discourse of the texts in correspondence with the new dogmatic conception or with the new problem proposed by the social transformations. In the field of the *Corpus Juris* it is possible to identify the historical product of two opposed mentalities that are stratified the one over the other: the first, responding to the needs of practicality and observant, in legislative politics, of the suggestions offered by the practice—this was the mentality proper of the Imperial Chancellery and that can be identified in the fifty *decisiones* in the *leges* of the Codex (as well as in *repetitae praelectionis*) and in the *Novellae*. The second, being absolutely doctrinal and tied to the models offered by the classic texts, is alimented in its archaicizing tendency by the re-elaboration of the *jura*,—is a mentality specifically of an élite of theoretical jurists, and can be found in the multiple historical residuals gathered in the Justinian Digesta.[166]

§ 42. Translation As An Art: Discovery Of An Adequate Rhythm And Style

The musical *discursus* of poetry presents particular difficulties to the task of translating. According to what has been previously underlined (*see GTI*, § 34.c. and § 39.c.), the musical discourse consists in the "resting the voice on the phonetic value (expressive) of the words that are sung, spelled, or read aloud, or at least read for people to hear, inserted in the musical phrase that is called 'the meter'.[167]"This leaning on the phonetic value is not intended only and not much for fashioning new phrases, but rather to awaken latent perspectives and emotive charges asleep in language,[168] bestowing on it significant pregnancy and distinctiveness. The translator of a poetic discourse must try to re-express its phonetic value in conjunction with the lyrical intuition, according to the different law and interior form of the language into which he wants to translate it. This task has been evidenced by the formula that U. Wilamowitz-Möllendorf proposed and Giovanni Pascoli substantially adopted.[169] "To translate, what is it?—what is outside must be renewed, what is within must remain the same as it is: the spirit remains, the body changes; the true translation is a phenomenon of metempsychosis." This formula is imaginary and metaphorical, to be understood *cum grano salis* and should not be trivialized; it is as if the linguistic original symbol was a sort of vest, that is possible to remove and change! Pascoli, who had a lot of experience in translations, said, "Translating is not to preserve in the classic work its spirit in a new physical reality, but to trans-form the least as possible its spirit; the trouble is that of choosing for the classic spirit a new vest that would make it appears different in the less possible way. When translating, we must observe the same proportion that exists in the text, of the thought with the form, of the inside with the outside." We must preserve in the poetic discourse, together with the lyrical power, also the phonetic value on which it is leaning. This presents the problem of discovering in the new language the rhythm and the style that better correspond to the rhythm and the style of the original ancient text. Only a superficial view may argue, from the intimate nexus between language and thought of the original poetic discourse, the absolute unbreakability that would make impossible and condemnable to an unsuccessful result, every attempt at a translation.[170] Whoever has some familiarity with problematics and with the inventive dedication of ingenious translators as A. W. Schlegel, U. Wilamowitz-Möllendorf, Giovanni Pascoli, Ettore Romagnoli, Vincenzo Errante, knows that the discovery of the adequate rhythm and style is not a point of impossible solution, even though it is a task of an extreme difficulty. Truly, even in the translation of the poetic discourse, what counts for the translation to be successful, is not the adherence of the words that usually are exchanged in faithfulness—as if they were per se gifted with a magic virtue to be grasped and captured, in the search for an impossible identity—but the correspondence of the meanings between the new representative form and the original one (*see GTI*, § 18). The translating interpretation, here too, must orientate itself toward the sense of the original discourse, and not toward an absurd equation of words. "Rem tene, verba sequentur" (Fix the thing in your mind, words will follow) is a criterion valid also here. Once the sense of the discourse is captured, the suitable words to re-express it come up spontaneously, according to the spirit and the laws of the language into which one is translating. This result—to re-express the sense of the discourse and not an abstract literal fidelity that is merely extrinsic[171]—must be the direct task of the translating interpreter, in the analogous manner as if it were a promoting result, not already an abstract, rigorous conformity to the so-called ethical law[172] is directed the task of the moral action.[173]

For the specific problematics that the translation of poetical works proposes, it may be instructive to know the succession of two phases through which it must go through: the first is focusing on the recognition of the meaning that has the greater adherence to the original text; the second, on the literary reproduction of the captivated meaning in the style better correspondent to the new language. These are operations that, in the case of works of theatre, can be trusted in the hands of different individuals according to the criterion of the greater competency. Very interesting, among others, is the confession of Fiammetta Moronti, to whom Ugo Betti consigned the task of preparing a translation into French of some of his plays: a French translation that would offer to the adaptor M. Clavel a text most faithful to the original text. Here is this confession.

> Everyone knows the insidious temptations of translating, knows that to remain faithful to the letter without betraying its spirit is a truly difficult thing, if there is no adhesion to the full inspiration and style of the author. Everyone knows that this demands an amorous dedication and an effort of comprehension that are not similar to that of a careful critical exegesis. This person knows also that, independently from the results of its own efforts, very few authors, especially dramatists, stand firm—at least in the secret conscience as translators—before this minute, inevitable, of any folding, any shading, any flection of the text. You have to know that Ugo Betti's text was—not only capable of resisting, but rather of imposing itself with the power of its most singular style—revealing to the meditative analysis a wideness of dimensions, a complexity and wealth of elements that, in part, can even escape—and, how often have they not escaped unfortunately to superficial, pressured, and prejudicial critics?!—in the rapid rhythm of the scenic performance.

An interesting confession this is. It confirms once more the possibility of reaching the lyrical power of the poetic discourse in its shadings, and predisposes to a sort of metempsychosis, both because in the screening of the required analysis of the hermeneutic process, the texts of an authentic poetry that distinguish and impose themselves with the weight of their unmistaken style from the texts of a minor consistence, in which the splendor of the form hides an irremediable lack of lyrical power: They will be texts that, under the translating operation do not resist and impose themselves. Here as elsewhere, in the process of the interpretive analysis, the light of inspiration and thought shines, or the text reveals its inconsistency. Thus the translator will be rewarded, as the reader, for its own dedicated task of intelligence—or will realize the delusion of an effort that has not reached its goal. The research of the adequate rhythm and style in the literary reproduction[174] depends essentially from the achievements of the intelligence of both, translator and reader.

APPENDIX
On the Problem of Translating

On this problem Horst Rüdiger, "The Problem of Translating," in *Vortragsreihe des Kaiser Wilhelms-Instituts für Kulturwissenschaft*, Heft 44 (Essen, 1943): a Lecture to which Betti was present, on 9 January 1943.

(8) What does it mean "to translate"? In recent times, three answers have been given that originated from fields fully diverse, and that coincide in their negativity: no true and proper translation exists. The first of the three answerers was Benedetto Croce, the second U. Wilamowitz-Möllendorf, and the third the French Germanist Geneviève Bianquis.

Wilamowitz says, "Put the letter away and follow the spirit; do not translate words or propositions, but take things within yourself and then render them in thoughts and sentiments. (9) The vest must become new, untouched the content. Every true translation is merely a change of the vest. To express myself in a manner more efficacious, let me say that the soul remains, the body changes. The true translation is metempsychosis."

Geneviève Bianquis, after her critical examination of J. F. Angelloz's translation of the *Duino Elegies*, says "One can change the words, vary the tone, imitate, but not translate." (10)

Three events concurred in shaking the open ingenuity of the translators and in focusing with a new clarity on the problematic character of their task.

(a) The first event originated from the profound consideration of original works, a consideration that reached its peak in the cult of the genius of the *Sturm und Drang*. What the translators, though negligently, translated at that time, was much estimated because, naturally, in it, the original genius was finding its expression. Thus, no longer they could sufficiently be well translated into a literary language already formed: it became necessary, in the translation, to recognize their individual and national character.

(b) The second event consisted of the philological criticism and of the modern historical consciousness: Vico and Herder had already prepared the field by underlining much clearly the singularity of the single geniuses and of the national genius; the great philologists of the age of Goethe also had sharpened the critical consciousness. (11)

(c) The third event that changed the attitude of the translators was caused by the poets. The passion of Klopstock for the ancient meter must have caused in the translators a kind of seduction, especially when an expert artist like Voss provided examples of the most difficult meters and the practice of exercises in the "Zeitmessung der deutschen Sprache" that gave, with fatal errors, a theoretical substrate to the movement. What Voss and his school did for ancient poetry, the Romantics did for the neo-Latin literatures. Meinhard and Carus, translating the *Divine Comedy* used in their essays the prose; others, among which Shelling, used free versification; but August Wilhelm Schlegel, Streckfuss, Kannegiesser, Schlosser, Gildemeister, George, and Falkenhausen, they all, tried their best to introduce the *terzina* in Germany. (12) However, the imitability of an ancient poetic meter or even modern, considered in themselves and per se, do not constitute yet the prove that they can be used in the translation of an original into German. What is decisive is that the style of the language of the translator, which comprehends also the meter, must correspond to the style of the original, that is, that the expression would substitute the other in so far as it is equivalent. The translator would do better, then, if he prefers to the illusory truth of an exact translation, the metempsychosis or the transposition with his own linguistic elements.

Following the historical inquiry, we arrived to the same result of the direct research: it is a pious illusion of historicism that the translator with a literal version or metric, only extrinsically exact (*a calco*), would be able to render also what constitutes the spiritual content of the original work.

The method of free or spontaneous versions in a literary style already formed cannot always give us the illusion of being before an original. (13) Wieland and Eschenburg translated Shakespear equally in prose. The dramas, however, so translated, exercised a decisive influence on the German literature and spiritual history in the last three decades of the 19th century. How profound this influence was is testified in *Poesia e Verità* (XI) by Goethe, who at the same time explicitly condemned the translations in verses. (14) In the notes and in the dissertations on the Divan, Goethe distinguishes three species of version:

> (a) "The first version makes us knowledgeable of foreign things according to our own mentality, and—to this purpose—the simple version in prose is the most idoneous. It is true that the prose eliminates all the peculiarities of any poetic art and lower at a common level the poetic enthusiasm itself, but, in compensation, it offers to us from the beginning the greatest service, it brings to us the best of what the foreign literatures in our national environment and in our common life can give, and, in an unconscious way for us, edifies us and procures a higher spiritual disposition. ....
>
> (b) Then comes a second period, in which we try to place ourselves in the conditions of life of the foreign country, but appropriating the foreign thought alone to make it as our own. Such period I would call it *parodist*, in the strictest literal sense of the word (15).... French people use this [method] in their translating any poetic work. .... French people, as they tend to assimilate foreign words to their own pronunciation, so they do also for the sentiments, and even for things. Thus, for every exotic fruit they demand absolutely a surrogate that must have grown on their land."

Goethe, then, defines the third method of translating as

> (c) "the one in which the will is of making a translation that is identical to the original and thus constitutes not a simple substitution (surrogate), but a true and proper reproduction. This manner of translating, at the beginning met with the strongest oppositions or resistances, because the translator, who limits itself to the text is renouncing more or less to the originality of his own national spirit. Thus, something different is born, to which it will be needed to educate the gusto of the multitude gradually and a little by little, in time."

This is what has been established: the cause of the aversion of Goethe for the translation in verses is, in the first place, of a pedagogical character; such translations are unsuitable because their form alienates the youth and the common people, "on which we must operate," from the spiritual content of the work. In perfect conformity with the spirit of his epoch, Goethe was defining as "supreme" the third method of translating: the historical-philological method. It is in this third period that the translators begin to render the poetic original in a poetic form. (16)

For us today, language is more than anything else the mediatory mean of the spirit: the spirit transmits ideas and concepts and is logically comprehensible. In the poetic language, the simple material instrumentality of tone and sound has per se a value that is not dissimilar from that of the musical creations: a value absolutely irreproducible through an imitation (Baratono, *Arte e Poesia*, 48, 70, 93). The poetical compositions, the value of which is particularly in the rhythm and in music cannot be translated neither in prose nor poetry, as it is for the same reason of a melody (the analogy does not hold because for the melody one can speak only of diverse interpretations that vary according to the personality and the conception of the interpreter). (17) These elements have an important part also in other kinds of poetry, but they do not constitute their decisive value. This means that the translator may still be able to render them poetically. In one case alone, which is after all at the true limit of the literary problematics, the translator will find himself in the true and proper impossibility of translating, as it happens for literary composition of a character eminently musical: in the translation of librettos of lyrical works. (18) From the dilemma of the translator of a libretto, it has practically resulted that either the transmitted texts did not care for the literal signification of the original, and thus paraphrased them, more or less, or the texts treated the German language as if the translators could use it as they wished. (19) The translator should not give up for this. It is precisely from recognizing the limits of their own activity that the true task will begin; task that consists in finding the style suitable to the originals and to the translators. (20) For sure, with the finding or elaborating of a style, the problem of translating can, in its essential part, be resolved. Truly, even then, it is impossible to avoid aporias, as when facing untranslatable words and poems, and the default of synonymy, etc., nevertheless fundamentally it can be said that even poems can be translated, if one could find the style that corresponds to them in the language of the translator. For this reason, many of the ancient spontaneous and free translations succeeded in resulting efficacious, because they reproduced candidly the original, in a literary style already formed; and again many successive translations did not succeed because deprived of the style, and beside that, they deluded because they bamboozled with the style of the original instead of transposing it.

"*To transpose*" a style means to find in the language of the translator a style that is appropriate and correspondent in its possible limits to the style of the original work. Often, however, a style may not manifestly appear in a certain language, and it will be necessary to discover and elaborate it. Every language, today, has a journalistic style, a scientific style, and a style for lecturing, etc. To chose then the exact linguistic category is more difficult than the *exact* translation itself. The style, deprived of a personal expressive value (21), for ex., a simple rendition, on whatever it may be, is in every language relatively poor and limited. It runs on tracks for a long time traversed and give no space to the free discovery and elaboration; every time someone ventures to overcome the consecrated limit of usage, risks to become ridiculous. Hence, it is possible to conclude that the translation of colorless texts could be more difficult than the translation of original texts that have an artistic value. The duty of translating begins with the investment of the creative power of language, when the translator must conquer a style, if there is no manifest style at all in his language. If, for ex., "to translate' could mean to reproduce the motion of the spirit regardless its stylistic particularities, this kind of translation would then have a senseless effect [apart always from the collaboration given by the listener]. (22) When for a specific literary kind no style already exists, then the translator has the great occasion of proving himself. He will not be strapped, as it happens in many specific categories of the language, by a tradition, to habits and usages; he would have, at his disposition, in his own language, an identical wealth of expressions—that the highest level of a language allows—as the poet in its original language. The translator must succeed efficaciously in its discovery and elaboration of a style, because he is also perfectly free.

This liberty always attracted the greater translators; because of it, they also translated poets. Naturally this freedom also has its own dangers. The translation can become so independent that the soft exotic breath no longer can be sensed, of which a trace should be found in every translation. One will believe then of being at home and of being guest one forgets. This period has been noticed only by translators of higher sensibility. Wilhelm v. Humboldt has observed that, "while the exotics and not the exoticisms are felt, the translation reaches its highest goal, but when the exoticism in se and per se is manifest, overcoming the exotics, then the translator shows of not being at the level of the original." (23) Humboldt believes that too much self-certainty is an obstacle to the true and proper translating because it nationalizes not only the form but also the foreign content, placing the exotic into a national style. The translation, says Humboldt, has the task of amplifying, by means of what is foreign, the language and the spirit of one's own nation. Translation is not for him a philological-metric problem, and even less a simple transference of content, but an educational task. (24) We must agree with Humbold that, by introducing the category of the exotic in the translation, which is itself a product of the method of conceiving pedagogy and culture, the danger of excessive freedom is eliminated during the creation by a translator of a style. What is decisive for the stylistic effort is the conscious stylization of the translation in sight of a determinate ideal, and not to be facing a linguistic incapacity. Schleiermacher, contemporary and as great as Humboldt, arrived at the same theoretical solution. (25) The problem consists in finding the way of expressing, in the language of the translator, the national spirit of another country, because such spirit is, as Herder taught, original and unrepeatable, and in its individuality exists its power. Schleiermacher exemplifies the dilemma in the following way: if he [Schleiermacher] could have translated the philosophical expressions of Plato in the philosophical terminology of his own time, then the impression could have been given that Plato possessed a philosophical terminology absolutely perfect. In order to avoid this vicious circle, Schleiermacher did not translate in the philosophical style of his time, but created for this purpose by himself a terminology. Schleiermacher wanted that the translator will "pass on also to the reader, to whom the translation is offered in its own language, the impression of being facing something exotic." (26) Though the solution of Schleiermacher seems quite utopist, the terms in which he put the question are correct. To translate and especially to translate poetic texts is a spiritual activity that is depending up to a certain point, but for the rest—and this is decisive—it is a free activity of the inventive spirit. Therefore, the question of the style of the translator cannot be resolve in a theoretical and objective manner, but every case by itself subjectively. The style of the translation is determined only by the personality of the translator, as the style of the original work depends from the personality of the poet. To Wilamowits, who revendicates only to the philologist the competence of translating Greek poetry, we must replicate with clarity that a Greek poem or in any other language can be done also by a philologist, who possesses a stylistic sense. The sensation of style is a gift more rare than linguistic knowledge and it cannot be acquired like the linguistic knowledge, but like the gusto and the touch belong to the innate dowry from nature. With this, we do not mean to refute the mediation of the philologist, as a competent linguistic interpreter: on the contrary, without its direct or indirect collaboration, no adequate translation would be made. (27) The fiction of the translator that would attend to his work as if it was an original is possible only by renouncing the illusion of an extrinsic similarity and with the consciousness of the limits of his activity. In this way, he will be able to have the liberty, which is necessary for finding or discovering and elaborating a style. The style is in function of the personality of a nation, of the historical epoch of the translator: it changes with the changing of these factors. Thus, to translate is also a task without end and it proves the perennial alive power of the original, if it reflects [shines], without ever losing its newness and beauty in the multiple and successive re-mirroring in other languages. Humboldt, who as a philosopher of language occupied himself about the problematics of translating, has recognized more clearly its value, when he wrote, "To translate, especially when translating poets, is one of the major and necessary duties in a literature, in part, in order to make those ignorant of foreign languages easierly approachable to forms of art and humanity that otherwise would remain unknown to them—from which every nation draws always notable advantages—but in part also, and specifically, because with that one accrues and benefits the expressive efficacy and the capacity of its own national language."

In the *Italianische Kulturnachrichten*, Nr. 43-48 (1955), p. XVIII, a new conference of H. Rüdiger on "DasUebersetzen als Stilproblem" is mentioned and an abstract is given.

With which intense sensibility the Romantic Age profoundly studied the problematics of translating also as a research of an adequate style has been underlined in the book of Madame De Stael, *De l'Allemagne*, chapter 18. The raw ingenuity of the modern scientific materialism brought this problematics back to its primitive terms of a rudimental communication by signs. In reference to this, N. Wiener, *Introduction to Cybernetics* (Italian translation, 1953, p. 22) said,

> It has been proven that the information is subject to a law analogous to that of entropy: a message in the process of transmission can lose spontaneously its own order, and would never be able to re-acquire it. For example, if in a telephonic conversation people are talking while there are disturbances of line, such to cause a considerable loss of power in the sent message, the person receiving it would not be able to understand some words and would be required to interpret them within the signification of the context... This happen also in the translation of a book from one language to another since it is impossible to render the exact meaning of the original, because between the two languages no precise equivalence exists. In these conditions, the translator has only two solutions: (a) uses some phrases that are more generic and vague than those in the original;

(b) modify the original by introducing a message that is not precisely that of the author and that possesses a signification diverse from that intended by the author to be given to his text. In both cases, something of the idea of the author will be lost."

This fact should never be dismissed that the given intention of the so-called exact sciences, when they are transferred on a land extraneous to them, they make us feel the disconsolate misery of reduction of spirituality to a quantitative dimension, without the most vague presentiment of what could *language* and *style* be (Baratono, Preface to Focillion, *La vita delle forme* (1945), 18-22).

End of chapter six or volume five of Betti GTI Series,
printed by CreateSpace & sold by Amazon, USA

The End of the First Chapter in the Second Volume of
E. Betti, *Teoria Generale dell'Interpretazione*, 1990
a cura di Giuliano Crifò

INDEX OF NAMES
[in the text alone]

Volume 1

Augustine, 76, 94
Bachofen, J. J., 70
Baratono, Adelchi, 21, 34, 50, 78
Bergson, H., 69, 87
Betti Lombardi, Gemma, 20
Betti, Ugo, 89
Buffon, G. L., de, 111
Bultmann, R., 19
Carducci, Giosuè, 89
Carnap, R., 79
Celsus, Publius Juventius (67-130 AD)
Cicero, 50, 51
Royer-Collard, P. P., 85
Crifò, Giuliano, 19-20
Croce, B., 29, 79, 98
Cunningham, G. W., 59
De Francisci, Pietro, 21
De Saussure, F., 75-76, 77, 79
Dilthey, W., 19, 94-96, 97
Dittrich, O., 77
Ducasse, C. J., 65
Eleatic, 32
Fabre, H., 69
Flacius, Matthias (1520-1575)
Freyer, Hans (1887-1969)
Gadamer, H. G., 19, 78
Giuffrè, Antonio (Publisher), 19
Goethe, W., 38, 68, 84
Hamann, J. G., 68
Hartmann, N., 22, 26, 79
Hegel, 21, 30, 32, 36, 37, 50, 96, 101
Herbart, Johann Friedrich (1776-1841), 30
Hofmann, J. Chr., 70
Hönigswald, R., 78
Humboldt, W., 46, 54, 78
Hume, D., 26
Husserl, E., 22, 77, 78, 83
Jespersen, O. 78
Kant(ian), 27, 28, 36,
Kant, I., 23, 25, 28, 29, 35, 41, 101
Klages, L., 57
Kreller, H., 22,
Lazarus, M., 30,
Leopardi, G., 69
Meyer, Knotterus, 69
Nietzsche, F., 22, 30, 31, 32, 56
Novalis, 68
Ogden, C. K., 59, 60, 61, 62, 63, 64, 65
Ortega y Gasset, J., 22

Pagliaro, A., 78
Pascal, B., 28, 94
Pascoli, G., 69
Peirce, Ch. S., 58, 59
Plato(nic/niz.), 27, 32, 33, 34, 35, 45
Plotinus
Richards, J. A., 59, 60, 61, 62, 63, 64, 65
Rothacker, E., 22
Royer-Collard, P. P., 85
Schelling, F. W., 68
Schleiermacher, F., 19, 69, 79, 82
Simmel, Georg (1858-1918)
Spinoza, B., 33, 40, 74
Spranger, E.,
Steinthal, H., 30
Tolman, 66
Uexküll, J. v., 71
Urban, W. M., 22, 78
Vico, G.B., 70
Vossler, K., 79
Weber, Max, 57, 58
Wittgenstein, 79
Wölffling, Heinrich (1864-1945), 57, 93

Volume 2

Anglo-Saxon, 101
Aristotelian, 42, 109
Aristotle, 57
Bacon, 87
Baratono, 25, 64, 111
Baroque, 93
Bentham, Jeremia, 46
Bernheim, E., 31
Böeckh, A., 69
Bollnow, O. F., 68, 69
Bruers, A. 31
Bultmann, R. 70
Byzantine, 93
Caesar, 69
Carducci, Giosue', 76-77
Carnelutti, F., 31
Celsus, Roman jurist, 99
Cicero, 79
Civil Italian Codex, 101
Conte, 31
Copernicus, 46
Croce, B., 32, 64
Darwin, C., 46
De Saussure, Ferdinand, 26, 27, 28
Demosthenes, 79
Descartes, R. 59

61

Dilthey, 66, 67, 71, 101
Droysen, 22, 31
Einstein, 31
Existentialism, 94
Existentialist, 115
Fantappiè, 31
Faust, 84
Ferrara, 31
Freud, 46
Freudian libido, 89
Freyer, Hans, 95
Gabor, Denis, 46
Galvani, 31, 75
Garboli, 31
Giuliano, 31
Goethe, 27, 82, 86, 112
Gothic, 93
Gozzoli, Benozzo, 64
Greek, 94
Gunther, G., 68
Hamann, 62
Harris, 112
Heidegger, 67, 68, 87
Herbart, Johann Friedrich, 98
Holderlin, 48
Homeric poems, 75
Humboldt, Wilhem, 22, 26, 27, 28, 46, 48, 49, 50, 76, 87, 105, 107, 112, 113
Husserl, E., 26, 27, 49, 53, 57, 59, 68, 75
Ipsen, G., 26
Jaspers, K., 69, 70
John, St., 107
Jolles, Andrè, 85
Jove, 61
Kant, 32, 43, 52, 55-56, 103
Kaufmann, F.Y., 68
Keller, Wilhelm, 68
Kelsen, H., 66
Lazarus, 44
Leibniz, G. W., 44
Lorenz, 31
Louis XIV, 88
Mac Dougal, 47
Matthew, St., 100
Milesi, 31
Misch, G., 69
Nietzsche, F., 48, 113
Novalis, 62
Ortega y Gasset, J., 48
Pareti, L., 31
Paul, Herman, 26
Paul, Saint, 86

Pawlow, I. P., 32
Phaedrus, 23
Plato, 23
Platonic, 105
Poe, Edgar Allan, 46
Proust, M., 86
Quintilian, 79
Renaissance, 93
Roman jurisprudence, 62
Roman Law, 108
Roman Priest, 61
Romantic comportment, 86
Romantic experience, 64
Russel, Bertrand, 33, 34
Schelling, G. W., 62
Schiller, F., 23, 55
Schleiermacher, F., 22, 78, 83, 95, 96, 101, 106, 107
Simmel, Georg, 93
Snell, B., 68
Socrates, 23
Socratic, 74
Somenzi, Vittorio, 46
Spinoza, B., 82
Urban, W. M., 89
Vaccarino, Giuseppe, 46
Volta, A., 31, 75
Weber, Max, 84, 85
Winckelmann, J., J., 112
Wölfflin, Heinrich, 97

Volume 3

Adler, M., 74
Aeschylus, 52
Alighieri, Dante, 44
Bacon, F., 59
Baratono, A., 54
Beuve, Sainte, 28
Bible, 44-45
Boeckh, A., 24, 34
Buddhism, 75
Burckhardt, Jacob (1818-1897), 74
Calvinistic, 74
Capitalism, 74
Cicero, 30
Copernican Revolution, 57
Croce, Benedetto, 25
Curtius, E. R., 69
Dante (*see* Alighieri)
De Sanctis, Francesco, 68
Dilthey, 69
Droysen, 60, 61
Dvorak, M., 69

Faust, 71
Goethe, 29, 35, 71
Gospel (Evangelium), 44
Grundmann, H., 71, 72
Hebrew Prophets, 75
Hecataeus of Miles, 51
Hellpach, W., 74
Hintze, 63, 64
Historian(s), 27, 28, 53, 57, 59, 67, 71, 74
Historicism, 64-67, 69
Homer, 44
Humboldt, 29, 63
Idealist(s), 49, 69
Illuminism, 63
Jäger, W., 69
Joachim of Fiore (d. 1202), 45, 71
Kant, 47, 57
Landor, W. S, 29
Martin, Alfred, 71, 72
Mephistopheles, 71
Nader, Joseph, 69
Nietzsche, 46
Nominalist(s), 49
Orientalist(s), 30
Otto Hintze (1861–1940)
Papirologist(s), 30
Pascoli, Giovanni, 44
Philologist(s), 34
Plato, 51, 70
Positivist(s), 8, 12, 49, 57, 63, 66, 69
Pragmatist(s), 61, 63
Preller, L., 25
Proesler, H., 74
Quintilian, 30
Rationalist(s), 46, 50, 78
Religion(s), 15, 64, 65, 67, 73, 75, 76
Rembrandt, 70
Robert, Carl, 25
Romanticism, 69
Scheler, 74
Schliermacher, 32, 38
Snell, Bruno, 69
Steinthal, H., 29
Troeltsch, E., 63, 64, 65, 66, 67
Upanishad, 75
Villani, Giovanni, 72
Weber, Max, 69
Welcker, Fr. G., 25
Wolf, Fr. A., 25

Vol. 4

16th Century, 139

17th Century
18th Century
19th Century
Abstractism, 63
Abstractism, 82
Addison, 38
Arc of Constantine, 65
Aristotle, 45, 100
Augustine, 83
Balzac, 99
Baratono, 44, 45, 58, 70, 76, 93, 94, 95
Baroque, 53, 54, 55, 56, 58
Bechtel, H., 137
Bellini, Giovanni, 49
Berenson, B., 36, 38, 40, 64, 74
Bergson, 38, 78, 79
Betti, Ugo, 76, 87
Blumenbach, 115
Boeckh, 31, 92-93,
Brentano, F., 79, 101
Brinkmann, C., 137
Giordano, Bruno, 41, 45
Brutus, 76
Buffon, 91
Byzantine art, 65
Caesar, 76
Calvinicm, 140
Canto 29° of Paradise, 87
Canto of the Angels, 87
Capitalism, 140
Carducci, Giosue', 70, 73, 95
Carsten, 62
Cervantes, 99
Cézanne, 61, 63, 81
Classic Values, 57
Classic, 55, 56, 57
Classicism, 55, 56, 57
Cohn, 45
contenutismo, 51
Croce, B., 29, 94, 96
cybernetics, 82
Dante, 73, 77, 84, 87, 99
De Sanctis, 87
De Saussure, 40
Dilthey, 32, 72, 78, 85, 86, 87, 90, 105, 120-121, 127
Diritto,105-125
Dossena, 81
Droysen, 105, 127
Dvorak, 48, 65
Egyptian art, 65
Eleatic, 58
Eleatic, Aristotelic or Kantian, 125

Index of Names

Eraclitus, 70
Ermatinger, Emil, 91
Erwin, Master, 36
Europe,
Expressionism, 55
Flaubert, 99
Frère Morieux, 82
Frey, Dag., 64
Freyer, H., 129, 132
Friedrich, D. C., 61
Fuente, Hans aus der, 40
Gardiner, 43
Gauguin, 61, 62
Giorgione, 48
Goethe, 127
Goethe, 35, 36, 37, 38, 43, 44, 45, 46, 47, 75, 76, 98, 99, 100, 116, 117
Gothic, 54, 56, 65
Goya, 62
Greek Civilization, 56
Gundolf, 44, 75
Hans Jakob Christoffel von Grimmels-hausen
Harris, J., 34, 35
Hartmann, N., 41, 45, 117
Hegel, 101, 117
Heidegger, 27
Hercules, 34
Herder, 35, 36, 138
Hermetism, 63, 82
Heussi, K., 141-142.
Hildebrand, Adolf, 49
History of Art, 57
Holderlin, 99
Humboldt, 38, 39, 40, 41, 42, 43, 45, 46, 58, 96, 124
Hume, 117
Husserl, E., 37, 79
Ibsen, 100
Idealism, 34
Ifigenia of Goethe, 100
Iliad, 97
Impressionism, 56, 61
Jhering, 107
Joachimi, M., 37, 45
Jolles, 115
Kant(ian), 58
Kant, 85, 104, 105, 120
Keller, G., 101
Kleist, 100
Koch, 36
Körner, Christian Gottfried, 46
Koschaker, 42
Krueger, Felix, 33

Lazarus, 123, 124
Leonardo, 70
Liberalism, 140
Lipps, H., 41
Manet, 61
Mannerism, 62
Marées, von Marées, 61
Medieval Art, 55
Meyer, Rich. M., 44
Michelangelo, 48
Middle Ages, 58, 137-140
Minor, J., 33
Monet, 61
Moritz, K. Ph., 45, 46
Müller-Armack, 135, 137
Naumburg, 63
Neo-Platonic, 34, 36, 38, 46, 65
Nietzsche, 36, 81
Nordic art, 65
Nordic sensibility, 55
Occidental Civilization, 56
Odessey, 97
Pagliaro, 38
Pawlow,
Perugino, 49
Peter Gynt, 100
Petersen, J., 41
Philippe Jacques de Loutherbourg, 82
Pinder, W. 59-63
Plato(nic), 40, 45, 52
Plato, 84
Plotinus, 33, 37, 45, 46
Pollaiuolo, 48
Pongs, 35, 45, 46
Porzig, W., 41
Prinz from Homburg, 100
Prometheus, 36
Pst-Classical, 55
Puritans, 138
Raphael, 49
Rembrandt, 63
Renaissance, 58, 65, 97
Ribot, T., 78
Rickert, 129
Riegl, Alois, 55, 135
Rilke, 95,
Romantic, 36, 45, 46, 51
Romanticism, 56
Rose, Hans, 55, 57
Rothacker, 26
Rubens, 62
Saenger, W., 41
Schäfer, 48

Schelling, 37,
Schiller, 35, 44, 45, 46
Schlegel, A. W., 36, 46
Schleiermacher, 25, 26, 29, 30, 36, 37, 44, 45, 69, 82, 101
Schwinger, R., 33, 34, 36, 37, 38, 41, 42, 43, 44, 45, 46, 47
Sebastiano del Piombo, 81
Seuffert, B., 45
Shaftesbury, 33, 34, 35, 45
Shakespeare, 76, 97, 100
Simmel, 37
Sombart, W, 133-140
Sömmering, 101
Spann, O., 137
Spiethoff, a., 137
Spoleto, 74
Spranger, 77
Staiger, 101
Stein, Fr., 34
Steinweg, 97
Stendhal, 99
Stern, W. 77
Stoic(s), 45
Stravinsky, 63
Strich, Fr., 33, 46
Technology
Tietze, H., 64
Titian, 49, 53
Triepel, 135
Tutmes in Tel-el-Amarna, 48
Uexküll, Jakob vom, 26, 45
Uhde, 61, 62
Unger, Rudolf, 90
Urban, 43
Verlaine, 78
Vico, G. B., 122, 127
Wagner, 67
Walzel, Osk., 33, 35, 97
Weber, Max, 118-119, 130-131, 137
Weippert, Willhelm, 137
Wieland, 36
Wilde, O., 54
Winckelmann, 34, 35, 38
Wölfflin, 49, 50, 51, 52, 54, 55, 91, 97
Worringer, W., 64

Vol. 5

"DasUebersetzen als Stilproblem,"58
"The Problem of Translating," 54
Angelloz, J.F., 54
Aristotle, 41, 48
Arte e Poesia, 56

Babel, 40
Baratono, 29, 33, 59
Baratono, 56
Baudelaire, 34
Bergson, 25
Betti, Ugo, 53
Bianquis, Geneviève, 54
canovaccio, 30, 39, 40
Carus, 54
Castle of Baia, 31
Clavel, M., 52
Constantine, 51
Corpus Juris Civilis, 50, 51
Croce, 31, 33, 34, 54
De l'Alemagne, 58
De Sanctis, 33
De Stael, Madame, 58
Digest, 26
Divan, 55
Divine Comedy, 54,
Duino Elegies, 54
duplex interpretatio, 50
Errante, Vincenzo, 52
Eschenburg, 55
Falkenhausen, 54
Fathers of the Church, 41
Focillion, 59
Freyer,, 50
George,54
Gildemeister, 54
glossema, 50
Goethe, 54, 55
Gospel of Matthew (15: 18, 24
Hegel, 40, 41, 42
Heine, 31
Herder, 54
Humboldt, W. ,32, 37, 57
Introduction to Cybernetics, 58
jargon,41, 42
Justinian Digesta, 51
Justinian Statutes, 48
Justinian, 51
Kannegiesser, 54
Klopstock, 54
La vita delle forme, 59
Meinhard, 54-
Melisande von Tripolis
Moronti, Fiammetta, 53
Morris, 42
Muller-Erzb, 42
Novellae, 51
Pascoli, Giovanni, 33, 52
Phenomenology of the Spirit, 40
Pirandello, 31, 32, 33

Plato, 41, 48
Poe, 34
Poesia e Verita', 55
Prince Charming, 25
Reiner Maria Rilke, 24, 34
Rem tene, verba sequentur, 52
Romagnoli, Ettore , 52
Roman Diritto, 50, 51
Rudel, Jaufré
Rüdiger., Horst , 54, 58
Schlegel, A. W., 52, 54
Schleiermacher, 57
Schlosser, 54
Scholastics, 41
Science of Logics, 40
Shakespear , 55
Sonnets of Orpheus, 24
Spinoza, 42
Streckfuss, 54
Sturm und Drang., 54
tabula rasa, 45
terzina, 54
translation-a-calco, 30, 39, 40, 55
Valéry, 34
Vico 54,
Voss, 54
Wagner, 25
Wieland, 55
Wiener, N., 58
Wilamowitz-Möllendorf, 33, 52, 54, 58

INDEX OF GERMAN TERMS IN PARENTHESES IN THE ITALIAN ORIGINAL TEXT

Vol. 1

abbildende, 77
An-sich-sein), 50
Aufbaugesetz, 73
Auffassungen, 77
bei den Sachen selbst
Dabei-sein, 83
das "Selbst"
  wiederverwirklichende
  Erinnerung, 83
des bewusstseinsmässigen Bei-ihm-
  selbst-seins, 83
deuten, 69
Deutung, 69
Dürken, 71
ein über-subjectivisch
  Seelisches, 57
erfahren, 88
Erfüllung, 77
erleben, 88
Erlebnis, 94
frei wovon, 56
frei wozu, 56
Gegen
Gehaüse, 71
glieder, 71
Grundbegriffe, 57
Hintergrund, 75
in der Weise des Selbsterfassten,
  Selbsgesehenen, 83
intentionale Leistung der
  Selbstgebung, 83
kunstgeschichtliche Grundbegriffe, 57
Schlagworte, 81
Seelisches), 57
Sein-für-Anderes, 50
selbstdarstellende, 77
Selbstgebung, 83
sich selbst verstehen, 72
Sinn vom Sein, 71
sinngeben, 69
Tonbild, 51
Ueberformung, 55
Umwelt, 72
Umwelten, 71
Uneinsichtigkeit, 56
Vergangen, 83
Vordergrund, 75
Wertgebilde, 73
Zeitlichkeit, 83
Zeitstelle, 83

Vol. 2

Abbildung, 37
abgebildet, 37
Ableitungsbegriff, 36
Angeschauten, 69
Aufarbeitung des Erkenntnisgutes,
  72
Auffassen, 69
Ausdruck, 57
Auseinandersetzung, 73
Ausspruch, 27
Bedeutungserfüllung, 57
Bedeutungsintention, 57
bei den Sachen selbst, 59
Bündigkeit, 111
das irgendwo von irgendwem
  Verstadene, 69
das Unverständliche, 70
Denken der Gemeinschaft, 30
denkend gegenwärtig, 69
Deutung, 37, 38
durch die nachgebildete Maske des
  Urverstehers, 86
eine gedankliche Bearbeitung des
  nur 'eingefühlten' Mit-oder
  Nacherlebens, 84
Einfälle, 79
Einfalt, 81
Einfühlung, 55, 83, 85
Einsicht, 68
Entsprechung, 24
erfassbar, 37
Erfassung, 61
Erfüllungseinheit, 58
Erlebnis, 57, 63
erlebte Rede, 50
Evidenz, 68
fliessend, 78
Folge, 36, 39
Folgebegriff, 36
Folgebeziehungen, 36
Formung, 85
Fremdverstehen, 68
Gedankeninhalt, 39
Gegenbild, 57
Gehalt, 36, 39
gehaltgleich, 36
gehaltgleich, 38
gehalttreue Uebersetzung, 37

gehalttreue, 37
Geistesgesch, 102
Gerede, 71
geschlossene Rede, 78
Geschlossenheit, 89
Gestalt,
gesunkenes Kulturgut, 81
Grundgedanken, 79
Inhalt, 36
inhaltliche Deutung, 36
Inhaltliche Redewise, 40
ins Bild setzen, 61
In-Sein, 67
Können, 113
Konstitutionssystem, 40
Lebensauffassung, 67
Lebensdeutung, 67
Lebenserfahrung, 67
Lebensverhältnis, 72
Lebensverständnis, 67
meinen, 27
Meinung, 27
Mit-sein mit anderen, 68
Mit-welt, 67
Mitwelt, 80
nachbilden, 83
nacherleben, 83
Nachversteher, 86
Nebengedanken, 79
Neo-Platonic, 112
ohne eigenes Erkennen, 69
Plotinus, 112
Rede-Antwort, 28
Reihenfolge, 38
richtig, 70
Rolle des Unverstehers, 86
Sätze, 35
Selbstgebung, Selbsthabe, 59
Selbstverständlichkeit, 86
Selbstverständnis, 68
Selbstverständnis, 69
Selbstverstehen, 68
sich einfühlen, 83
Sichverstehen, 68
Sichverstehen, 68
Sinnbegriffe, 38
sinngebendes Erlebnis, 58
Sinngebung, 72, 74, 94
sinngemässe Uebersetzung, 37
Sinnlogik, 39
Sinnzusammenhang, 102
Sprachsinn, 112
stimmen gehaltmässig überein, 37
Teilhabe, 94

Teilsätze, 38
Teilsprachen, 37
Uebereinstimmung, 36
Umdeutung, 116
umkehrbar, 37
Urversteher, 86
Verschlossenheit, 89
verstehen das Verstandene, 69
Verstehen des Verstandenen, 70
viel näher dem Erleben, 86
Vorstellungsinhalt, 39
Vortrag, 79
Vorverständnis, 67
weil es ein unendliches der
    Vergagenheit und Zukunft ist,
    was wir in dem Moment der
    Rede sehen wollen, 83
Wert-antwort, 94
wertbeziehende Interpretation, 85
Wertgefühle, 84
Wiedererinnerung, 59
Wiedererinnerung, 68
wirkende Gestalt, 81
wirklichkeitsloses Verstehen, 70
Wollen, 113
Woraufhin der Befragung, 72
Worthaftigkeit des Denkens, 42
zeichen- od. ausdruckswise
    Uebersetzung, 37
Zuordnung, 37
Zusammenhang des Sinnes, 93
Zweitakt, 60

Vol. 3

Ausdruckspsychologie, 34
Bekenntnis, 50
Darstellung, 26
Erkenntnis, 50
Geistesgeschichte, 70
im Befolgen einer Reihenfolge, 32
Kultur, 63
Kulturgeschichte, 70, 74
Masstäbe, 63
Mythe, 50
Nacheinander
Naturdeutung, 50
Seinskultur, 71
Sinnbild, 51
Sprachwerdung, 27
Ueberreste, 54
Umwelt, 53

vorlesen, 27, 39

Vol. 4

(das Gemüth ergreifen, 43
Abbild, 34
abgewandelt, 40
Ablaufsgesetze, 119
Absicht, 71
Angesprochensein, 99
Anhauch, 40
auf dem Rhein, 101
Aufbaugesetze, 119
Auffassung, 42
Ausführung, 37
aus-schliessend beschränkender Begränzung, 42
Bahn, 41
Besonnenheit, 36
Bündigkeit, 27
Dauer in Wechsel, 101
die Zeit geht nicht, 101
Einbildungskraft, 39 , 40
eingefallen, 82
einmalig, 40
Erfinden u. Entdecken, 26
Erlebnis, 71
Erregung, 37
Erwirken, 79
Erzählhaltungen, 99
Erzählungsweisen, 99
Fabel, 71
fasst, 39
formende Gesetzlichkeit, 32
Formerlebnis, 46
Formgefühl, 54
Ganzheit, 45, 127
Gattungsbegriffen, 43
Gattungsformen, 45
Gefüge, 99
Gehalt, 35, 71
Geistesrichtung, 38
geistige Gesamhaltung, 135
geistiger Einheit, 42
Gemeingeist, 134
Gemeinsamkeit, 134
Gesamtsinn, 138
Gesetzlichkeit, 118
Gesinnung, 139
Gestalt, 33, 35, 62, 71
Gestaltidee, 133
Ineinsbildung, 40

innerliche Vorbildung, 37
Kitsch, 63
Können, 27, 64
Kräfte, 56
Kulturleben, 135
Kulturstil, 135
Kunst-Wollen, 64
Laut-Analogie, 40
Lautform, 38
Lautverbindungen, 40
Lebensansicht, 86
Lebensdeutung, 85, 87
Lebensgefühl, 86
Mehrfugigkeit, 135
nie endender Bestimmbarkeit, 39
Problemgeschichte, 86
produktiver Einfall, 26
rein umschreibend, 42
Richtung, 42
seelisches Keimbläschen, 36
Selbstdarstellung, 71
Sinnädaquanz, 135, 136
sinngemässe Korrelationen, 119
Sinngesetze, 119
Sinnstruktur des prägenden Geistes, 135
sinnvolle Einheit, 133
Sprachkraft, 43
Sprachsinn, 38
Sprachsphäre, 43
Stimmung, 71
Structurgesetze, 119
Strukturepsychologie, 77
sunder warumbe, 102
todte Masse, 42
Ueberkommenes, 42
Umsicht, 101
Unbekanntes, 40
Urphänomen, 134
Urteilskraft, 39
Vermögen, 42
völkischer Geist, 134
vorbildende Besinnung, 36
Vorstellungsbestand, 82
Wandlung des zentralen Weltbildes, 139
Weg, 42
Wertforschung, 57
Wirkungszusammenhang, 120
Wirtschaftsgesinnung, 133
Wirtschaftssystem, 133

Wirtschaftsweise, 133
worumwillen, 102
Zeitgeist, 134
Zusammenhang, 38

Vol. 5

Ansichsein, 42
Auffasslichkeit, 24
aufheben, 35
Bündigkeit, 27
Deutung, 47
Dolmetscher, 36, 38
Fürsichsein, 42
Geräte des Lebens, 50
Interessenlage, 42
Machtlage, 42
Umdeutung, 48, 51
Zeitmessung der deutschen Sprache, 54
"das geheimste, mirselber, in ihrem Aufkommen und sich-mir-Autragen, rätselhafteste Diktat,"
"diese Gedichte, vorlesend, genau mitzuteilen," 24

ENDNOTES

[1] Published as "Methode und Wert des heutigen Studiums des Römischen Rechts" in *Tijdschr voor Rechtsgessch*. XV (1937), 137-174.

[2] Published in *Riv, int. fil. dir.*, xxvi (1949), 1-38.

[3] The scheme is in *Riv. Ital. Scienze Giuridiche* (1948), 86-91; and, a little changed, in *Interpretazione della Legge*, pp. vi-x. Adelchi Baratono (Firenze, 8 April 1875 – Genova, 28 September 1947) was an Italian philosopher and politician, one of the most important exponents of the Italian Socialist Party in between the two World Wars.

[4] Published in a booklet by itself and then incorporated in *Riv. Ital. Scienze Giuridiche* (1948), 34-86.

[5] This book published by Giuffrè (1949) constitutes the Chapter 8 of the present *General Theory of Interpretation*. It is also in *Zschr. (oest.) f. öff. R.*, 1950, 138-143.

[6] Published in the *Acts of the Congress* (1951, vol. ii, 103-120).

[7] A review was made on the *Triepel* in *Annuario dir. compar.* xxv (1950), 318-322.

[8] Conference edited in *Archiv f. Rechts- u. Sozialphil.* xl (1952) 354-374; in *Europa and Diritto Romano* (Studi Koschaker), vol. II, 441-460.

[9] Published in *Deutsche Vierteljahreschrift f. Literaturwiss. u. Geistegessch.* xxvii (1953), 489-508.

[10] As in the contribution to the *Studies* in honor of Albertario (II, 421; Arangio Ruiz (iv, 81); De Francisci (I, 133); in the conference Wesen des altröm. Familienverbands (25 May 1951), in *Zschr. d. Sav. St.*, 71 (1954), 1-24.

[11] See in *Riv. Ital. Scienze Giuridiche* (1951) together with a review of Kreller in *Oesterreich. Zschr. f. offentl. Recht* (1950), 138. This review has the value of being the first attempt to a criticism of our ideas. Pietro De Francisci (Roma, 18 December 1883 – Formia, 31 January 1971) was an Italian jurist, academician and political figure. He had been the Minister of Grace and Justice in the Government of Benito Mussolini.

[12] See my *Notazioni autobiografiche* (Cedam, 1952), 49-53.

[13] This is as much as Betti says about himself, but he was proud of having created the "Institute of the Theory of Interpretation." This is what he wrote about it: "The theory of interpretation (or hermeneutic theory) is a theory that interests all the "sciences of the spirit," in its largest extension of meaning (mind), and constitutes a conspicuous part of the relative methodology. It also concerns some reproductive arts (like those described at the letter /g/ here below). The theory of interpretation particularly concerns itself with the following branches of knowledge: (a) linguistics and semiotics, psychology and psycho-technology (pedagogy); (b) philology and history of literature, history of the arts, logic syntax of language, and history of the sciences; (c) history (historical methodology, history of right, history of the juridical dogmas and doctrines; (d) sociology (sociological methodology), history of economic and social formation; (e) jurisprudence (hermeneutics of law), comparative rights, and private international rights; (f) theology and canonic rights (hermeneutics of faith); in addition, (g) methodics of translations, dramatic and musical interpretation. In the contemporary structure of the academic studies, a teaching of hermeneutic theory does not exist, neither as a general theory of interpretation nor as special theory of the hermeneutic

methodology. Such methodology, however, is taught within the orbit of each specific science. Nevertheless, it would be for the superior interest of a synthesis to try to remedy the disadvantages of the contemporary specialization within the vast field of the sciences of the spirit with the elaboration of an hermeneutic theory. This theory — that should have character of science, and not of philosophy, should not be adept to any particular philosophical system — should study the epistemological problem of understanding (which is the precise modality of the problem of knowing), and especially the hermeneutic methodology, clarifying the common and differential aspects that the hermeneutic method assumes in the various fields of knowledge."

[14] In this last sentence the poet Ugo Betti is remembered, Emilio's younger brother.

[15] Schleiermacher, *Hermeneutik*, parla piu' spesso di "machkonstruieren" (17, 20, 32, 96, 215), ma anche di "nachbilden" (39): *Reden u. Abhandlungen*, in *Werke*, III Abt. III, 297, 358) o di "nacherfinden" (*Hermen.*, 214). Di "nachbilden", di "erleben" e "nacherleben" parlano, in epoca piu' recente , Dilthey, *Gesammelte Schriften*, V, 263-264; VII, 224 sg., e Simmel, *Probleme der Geschichtsphil.*, 4a ed., 77. Di "inneres nachershaffen" parla R. Unger, *Aufs. zur Prinzipienlehre der Literaturgesch.* (1929), 30. Come riproduzione interiore concepisce l'intendere anche Droysen, Historik, § 9: 328, quando nota che l'altrui manifestazione, proiettandosi nell'interiorita' di chi la percepisce, vi provoca il medesimo processo interno (cfr. Wach, *Verstehen*, III, 166; per la differenza dalla imitazione, A Jolles, *Einfache Formen*, 36 sgg: "nacheifernd abbilden"; Snell, *D. Aufbau der Spracke*, 20, e nota, ove si precisa la differenza fra il rappresentare intenzionale (imitare) e la funzione semantica che la parola adempie nel presentare e nel rappresentare l'oggetto; Porzig, *Wunder der Sprache*, 347 sg.). Qualificano in senso tecnico l'interpretazione riproduttiva quale "nachschaffendes (reproduzierendes) Künstlertum":Fr. Stein, Die Kunst der Rechtsprechung, 1900, 35 sg., e W. Jellinek, Gesetz, Gesetzesanwendung, Zweckmässigkeitserwägung, 1913, 169, n. 36-37; Furtwängler, Gespräche über Musik, 1948, 19: 2 A., 18.

[16] Dilthey, *Ges. Schr.*, V, 265; VII, 120, che parla di un "zurückübertragen."

[17] Humboldt, Werke, VII, 56 sg. ("natürlich, das eben Verstandene gleich wieder aus zusprechen"); Segond, *Traité de psichologie*, 184; cfr. Carnelutti, *Meditazioni*, I, 1942, 139-143, che trova espressa l'essenza dell'intendere nell'*intelligere*, quasi "intus legere" (140) e afferma l'esigenza che "l'interprete sia prima di tutto un lettore, e cosi' ricrei, o meglio riviva l'opera poetica o, insomma, riempia il bianco-segno": giacche altrimenti "sarebbe solamente, a guisa di fonografo, un trasmettitore."

[18] Che la rappresentazione letteraria di una interpretazione filologica, o storica, o tecnica, sia essentzialmente, per l'interprete, un rappresentare a se stesso il processo ermenutico tenuto e il risultato raggiunto, e solo per vis di conseguenza unrappresentarli per altri (in funzione didattica), discende dalla natura stessa del linguaggio: il quale, prima (logicamente) di divenire strumento di comunicazione, e' condizione del pensiero. Non bisogna dimenticare neppure a questo proposito il grande insegnamento did

Humboldt, *Werke*, VI, 155: "ohne irgend auf die Mittheilung zwischen Menschen und Menschen zu sehen, ist das Sprechen eine nothwendige *Bedingung des Denkens* des Einzelnen in abgeschlossener Einsamkeit."Vero e', (soggiunge Humboldt) che nella sua fenomenologia lo svolgimento della lingua ha luogo solo nell'ambiente sociale, e che l'uomo arriva a intendere se stesso proprio col saggiare negli altri la intelligibilita' delle sue parole. Gli e' che l'oggettivita' del linguaggio si potenzia, quando la parola che l'uno ha foggiato riecheggia dalla bocca dell'altro, suo interlocutore; ma con questo non e' tolto nulla alla soggettivita' del suo legame col pensiero: perche' l'essere umano si sente sempre unito in corrispondenza di sensi con altri esseri umani, e cosi' si potenzia anche quella soggettivita' dal momento che la rappresentazione (idea) tradotta in linguaggio non appartiene piu' esclusivamente ad un solo soggetto. La rappresentazione del processo e risultato ermeneutico diventa, dunque, attraverso la funzione comunicativa e didattica che assume, patrimonio di tutti. Ma non si puo' dire che questo ulteriore guadagno sia nella sua destinazione. D'altronde sono possibili altre ipotesi, nelle quali la traduzione della interpretazione in linguaggio non avviene: cosi', nell'interpretazione che l'interlocutore fa del discorso che ascolta, o in quello che si opera in *interiore homine* nella ricognizione dei propri ricordi.

[19] Contro la definizione proposta dall'Ernesti (*Institutio interpretis*, 7-8), "est interpretatio facultas docendi, quae cuiusque orationis sententia subiecta sit: interpretatio igitur omnis duabus rebus continetur, sententiarum verbis subjectarum intellectu, earumque idonea explicatione," ha bene osservato Schleiermacher, *Hermeneutik*, 7, che l'ermeneutica (non in quanto teoria, ma in quanto arte dell'interpretazione) e' soltanto arte dell'intendere, e non abbraccia anche l'esposizione dell'intendimento raggiunto: "nur Kunst des Verstehens, nicht auch der Darlegung des Verständnisses." Senonche' dopo questa esatta messa a punto, taluni han continuato a confondere l'intendere con l'esposizione che se ne fa, e a non rilevare l'estrinsecita' dello scopo didttico (cui serve l'esposizione del risultato raggiunto) rispetto all'attivita' interpretativa alla quale puo' accompagnarsi. Cosi', il Croce, *La Poesia*, 2a ed., 127; cosi' anche il Carnelutti, *Meditazioni*, I, 144, che qualifica in senso pregnante "arte anche l'interpretazione, ma secondaria o complementare: arte dell'arte nel senso che presuppone unarte prima di essa allo stesso modo che questa presuppone la natura" (arte, dunque, esteriormente riproductiva). E cosi', da ultimo, il Maggiore, "Interpretazione, etc.," in *Rivista penale*, 1949, 228-231, spec. 229. Basta qui aver segnalato la genesi di questo errore di prospettiva, con cui si ricade nella vecchia nozione dell'Ernesti, gia' criticata e superata da Schleiermacher.

[20] Sulla esigenza di fedelta', che vale per il tradurre come per ogni decifrare e riprodurre, si pronuncia Jacob Grimm a proposito della riproduzione di poesia di natura (che egli ritiene nettamente differente dalla poesia d'arte), nell'epistolario con Armin ("Achim von Armin und Wilhelm Grimm, barbeitet von Reinhold Steig," 255, riferito in Jolles, *Einfache Formen*, 226), nei termini seguenti: "Wir kommen hier auf die Treue. Eine mathematische ist vollends unmöglich und selbst in der wahrsten, stregsten Geschichte nicht vorhanden; allein das thut nichts, denn dass *Treue* etwas wahres ist, kein

Schein, das fuhlen wir und darum steht ihr auch eine *Untreue* wirklich entgegen. Du kanst nichts vollkommen angemessen erzählen, so wenig du ein Ei ausschlagen kannst, ohne dass nicht Eierweiss an den Schalen kleben bliebe; das ist die Folge alles menschlichen und die Façon, die immer anders wird. Die rechte Treue wäre mir nach diesen Bild, dass ich den Dotter nicht zerbräche. Bezweilfest du die Treue unseres Marchenbuches, so darfst du die letztere nicht bezweifeln, denn sie ist da. Was jene unmögliche angeht, so würde ein anderer und wir selbst grossentheils mit andern Worten nochmals erzählt haben und doch nicht minder treu, in der Sache ist durchaus nichts zugesetzt oder anders gewendet."

[21] La differenza e' notata da Furtwängler, *Gespräche über Musik*, 1948, 9, e gia' dal Parente, *La musica e le arti*, 1936, 218 sg., il quale ultimo, pero', cade nell'errore di una prospettiva ingenuamente oggettivistica, allorche' afferma che per chi ha occhi e coscienza "una statua o un quadro sono per se stessi (!) vive e parlanti creature," dimenticando e l'impegno richiesto anche qui alla spontaneita' del soggetto contemplante e la sua peculiare maniera di mirare (Hartmann, *Problem d. geist. S.*, 421 sg.; cfr. Marangoni, *Saper vedere*, 1933; Baratono, *Prima grammatica*, 2a ed., 252-256; Focillon, *Vita delle forme*, 97-116; 139-149; cfr. prolegomeni (*see GTI*, § 8.a.).

[22] Cfr. Parente, *Musica*, cit. 219. Sul problema filologico della lettura e ricostruzione del testo musicale, inter. A. Piovesan, "Validita' del testo vivaldiano" (in *Radiorcorriere*, 1-5-1949), circa i limiti di legittimita' della trascrizione.

[23] Cfr. Parente, *Musica*, 216. Sulla latitudine lasciata dalla non univocita' dell'opera d'arte, Hartmann, *Problem*, 424 sg.

[24] Contro tale tendenza storicistica, Furtwängler, *Gespräche über Musik*, 100 sg.; inter. Mich. Lessona, "Nel mondo della musica" (in Radiotrasmissione, 31-12-1948).

[25] Su questo analogo problema, Stanislawski, *An actor prepares*, 1936, 278 sg.

[26] Cfr. Romano, *Corso amministrativo*, 1930, 145 sg; Herrnritt, *Grundlehren d. Verwaltungsr.*, 1921, 294 (nota), 299 sg.; M. S. Giannini, *Potere discrezionale*, 52 sg.; nostra "Interpretazione della legge," 58 sgg.; *Dt. Vierteljahresschr. f. Lit. wiss. u. Geistegesch.*, 27, 507.

[27] Cio' riconosce, non senza incoerenza con la propria tesi, anche il Parente, *La musica e le arti*, 1936, 217, 221.

[28] Cosi', Parente, *La musica e le arti*, 218, identificando il compito dell'interprete nel "ripristinare le condizioni fisiche indispensabili alla comunicazione" dell'opera d'arte (220 sg): còmpito che egli qualifica "funzione pratica e non lirica, ed insomma tecnica, non creativa" (223). Errore codesto determinato da una premessa atomistica, identificabile nella concezione crociana che scinde la sintesi ermeneutica dal lavoro preparatorio, di carattere pratico, al quale spetta il puro "ufficio di stimolo al ricordo": modesto ufficio, che il Croce ravvisa conferito all'esecutore musicale (*La poesia*, 2a ed., 280, concorde col Parente), come –in altro campo – al traduttore (*Quaderni di Critica*, N. 13, mar. 1949, 88 sg.; cfr. *Estetica*, 5a ed., 76; *La poesia*, 279 sg.; in senso contrario nostro rilievo in *Interpretazione della legge*, 180, nota 40) e persino al filologo: il còmpito del quale, a suo avviso (*Quaderni di Critica*, N. 15, novembre 1949, 96 sg.), sarebbe

unicamente quello di "raccoglier e curare la buona conservazione del materiale utile all'indagine storica," mentre spetterebbe allo storico di congiungere la categoria ermeneutica con l' "elemento sensitivo o intuitivo" consistente nel "documento vivo da interpretare" [contro questo modo di vedere (see GTI, § ??); Righi, in Dolta, 1950]. Qui basti aver segnalato la genesi dell'errore del Parente dalla atomistica premessa crociana che, disconoscendo la totalita' spirituale dell'interprete, cui e' affidata la interpretazione riproduttiva, ne abbassa il còmpito a una funzione "tecnica" d'indole meramente pratica.

[29] Cfr. Lehmann, *Droit de l'artiste*, 1935, 167; Hanslick, *Vom Musikalisch-Schönen*, 6a ed., 1881, 112-114.

[30] Cosi', Parente, La musica etc., 220-224. Nell'opposto ordine di idee, Hanslik, op. cit., 112-114; Furtwängler, *Gespräche über Musik*, 35 sg., 2a ed., 33 sg.

[31] Nel qual senso soltanto e' esatta la qualifica di "arte secondaria o complementare" proposta da Carnelutti, *Meditazioni*, I, 144 sg.

[32] Baratono, *Prima grammatica*, 2a ed., 345 che qualifica l'interpretazione "arte sopra l'arte," nella quale l'interprete fa rivivere l'opera originale attraverso la propria ispirazione; Furtwängler, *Gespräche über Musik*, 19, pone la "Verwandlungsfähigkeit" come requisito fondamentale del "nachschaffendes Künstlertum."

[33] D'Amico, ne *L'arte dell'attore*, ed. Chiarini e Barbaro (1950), 120-140, spec. 125.

[33] Baratono, *Arte e poesia*, 48.

Arte e poesia, 48

[35] Ad. Müller, *Zwölf Reden über die Beredsamkeit*, 53; cfr. 6 sgg.

[36] Su cio', da ultimo, Kip H. G., *Das sogen. Mündlichkeitsprinzip*, 1952, 117 sgg.; G. Foschini, in *Scritti giuridici in onore di V. Manzini* (1954), 215-216, sul contradditorio come convincimento dei giudicanti.

[37] Baratono, *Arte e poesia*, 47.

[38] Da Baratono, *Arte e poesia*, 110-111.

[39] Rilke, *Briefe*, II (1914-1926), ed. K. Altheim, nr. 385; lettera diretta a Xaver von Moos, in data 20 aprile 1923; Ugo Betti, nelle testimonianze di A. Perrini, in *Fiera Letteraria*, 21 giugno 1953 (n. 25).

[40] Ad. Müller, *Zwölf Reden üb. d. Beredsamkeit*, 19.

[41] Ad. Müller, *Zwölf Reden üb. d. Beredsamkeit*, 52-53; Cfr. Tamberlani, *Tecnica dell'espressione nell'azione parlata e scritta*, 1954, 29 sg., 61 sg.

[42] In proposito, vedi P. Abraham, "Interpretation, " in *Encyclopédie française*, XVII, 1760-1761.

[43] Cfr. Hartmann, *Problem d. geist S.*, 439; Parente, *La musica e le arti*, 218-219; dissenziente, Graziosi, in *Rassegna musicale*, 1938, 193 sg.; Pugliatti, *Interpretazione*, 67 sg.

[44] Per siffatto strumento di deposito e non gia' per il disco, calza il paragone, musica "in conserva": E. Vuillermoz, in in *Encyclopédie française*, XVI, 1688, 7. Il Calogero, *Estetica, istorica, semantica*, 135 sg. parla di un "impoverimento della registrazione" che fa assegnamento sulla capacita' ricreatrice dell'interpretazione.

[45] Il parallelismo fra regista e direttore d'orchestra e' avvertito da G. Graziosi, in *Rassegna musicale*, 1938, 211-212; concorde, Pugliatti, *Interpretazione musicale*, 1940, 111 sg.

[46] Graziosi, in *Rassegna musicale*, 1938, 212;

[47] Graziosi, in *Rassegna musicale*, 1938, 197; 214.

[48] Cfr. J. Arnaud, *Charles Dullin*, 1952, 96, 170-174, 224.

[49] Humboldt, *Werke*, VII, 177 sg.; Winckelmann, in Heinr. v. Stein, *Die Entstehung der neuren Aesthetik*, 1886, 185: "indem sich ein Haupt vor meinem Auge erhebt, fangen in meinem Gedanken die übrigen mangelhaften Glieder sich an zu bilden: es sammelt sich ein Ausfluss aus dem Gegenwärtigen und wirkt gleichsam eine plötzliche Ergänsung." Vedi anche Winckelmann, *Ewiges Griechentum* (1943), 53.

[50] Da N. Hartmann, *Problem d. geist. S.*, 421, e' messo in rilievo "der hohe-Grad der Individualisierung, die das Spiel der Gestalt verleiht"; 425.

[51] Cosi', Parente, *La musica e le arti*, 1936, 223.

[52] Cosi', Parente, *La musica*, 221-222.

[53] Dal Furtwängler, *Gespräche über Musik*, 2a ed., 62-64 ("Geisted der Improvisation"); Cfr. in quest'ordine d'idee, Baratono, *Arte e poesia*, 74-76. Veramente l'insegnamento del Furtwängler e' in contrasto con la moda di oggi.

[54] Nel linguaggio di Peirce, *Collected papers*, I (1931), § 564, citato in Morris, *Signs, language and behavior*, 1946, 289-290, la chiave interpretativa si direbbe lo "interpretant" – riconosciuto *a parte subiecti* --- della forma rappresentativa, che il Peirce denomina "representamen." Sopra, (*see GTI*, § 1.c.).

[55] Per la concezione qui sostenuta cfr. specialmente Furtwängler, *Gespräche über Musik*, 2a ed., 11, 28 sg., 56 sg., 71, con energica accentuazione della funzione strumentale del materiale espressivo rispetto al contenuto d'anima (Seelisches) dettato "unter dem Gesetz der Improvisation" (ivi, 62). Si richiama qui quanto si e' esposti sopra, (*see GTI*, § 33.a.).

[56] Confonde l'uno con l'altro piano, negando in definitiva il vincolo di subordinazione dell'interprete, il Pugliatti, *Interpretazione musicale* (1940), 36, 48, 52.

[57] Per una netta differenziazione fra interpret storico dell'arte e interprete chiamato a riesprimere cfr. Furtwängler, *Gespräche über Musik*, 2a ed., 99-100, che caratterizza l'atteggiamento dell'uno (lo storico) siccome rivolto a dominare lo svolgimento dell'arte e a compararne le forme e fli stili, e quello dell'altro siccome soggiogato da devozione e amore per l'opera da riesprimere. In questo indirizzo si potrebbe adattare al primo "cum grano salis" la qualifica usata da Nietzsche, *Menschl. Allzumenschl.*, I, 327, di "don Giovanni della conoscenza" e dire che gli manca quello specifico amore potenziato che e', invece necessario al secondo. Di qui anche la "convertibilita'" dell'ermeneutica storica con l'istrumentario dogmatico, accentuato dal Rothacker, *Die dogmatische Denkform*, 259: sopra, (*see GTI*, § 13.a.).

[58] Baratono, *Il mio paradosso*, 24.

[59] Sulle esigenze della dizione, Furtwängler, *Gespräche über Musik*, 2a ed., 102 sg. Osserva il Dullin (*Souvenir d'un acteur*, 107 sg.) che pochi attori sanno

dire i versi senza involgarirne il ritmo e, cosi', snaturarne il senso e lo spirito: quasi tutti si lasciano trascinare a quella cadenza monotona che induce l'automatismo della cesura nell'allessandrino e impongono il medesimo automatismo alla prosodia moderna declamando tutti i poeti alla stessa maniera. La ragione profonda di codesto malinteso sta nel disconoscere che per la retta dizione del verso occorre risentirne la liricita' da poeta (ressentir en poète): onde, quando si tratta di poesia pura, e' difficile insegnare la giusta dizione, mentre quando si tratta di declamazione lirica nella tragedia, si puo' arrivare col dovuto impegno a trovare l'unita' di tono necessaria in tutti gli attori che partecipano alla rappresentazione. Vero e' che anche qui la tradizione, attraverso le interpolatzioni, si e' involgarita. Qui la passione dovrebbe provocare un'esaltazione interiore tanto nell'attore quanto nello spettatore: dovrebbe risvegliare in noi la coscienza, scuotere l'apatia, strapparci a forza alla quotidianita' e alla sua trasandatezza. Cfr. D'Amico, in *Arte dell'attore*, 1950, 120-140.

[60] Quello che il Rothacker, *Die dogmatische Denkform*, 261, chiama "den inersten Logos des Werkes."

[61] Cfr. Fr. A. Wolf, *Vorlesungen über die Encycl. d. Altertumswiss.*, hgg. von Gurtler, 1832 (= Kleine Schriften, II, 826 sgg.): Wach, *Verstehen*, I, 68, n. 2; Boeck, *Methodologie*, 2a ed., 158-162.

Sui problemi del tradurre vedi Schleiermacher, "Ueber die Verschiedenen Arten des Uebertsetzens," comunicazione all'Akademie der Wissenschaften zu Berlin, del 24 giugno 1813, *Werke*, III, Abt. II, 207-245; Goethe,*Wahrheit und Dichtung*, libro XI, a proposito della traduzione di Shakespear del Wieland; Novalis to A. W. Schlegel, 30 novembre 1797; Wilamowitz-Möllendorf, "Was ist Uebersetzen?" (pref. all'Ippolito, 1891), in *Reden u. Vorträge*, 3a ed., 1913, 1-29. Per una traduzione italiana della fenomenologia e logica di Hegel, in *Rendiconti Istituto Lombardo*, 1941-1942, fasc. 2; H. Rüdiger, *Problemi del tradurre*, 1943; nostra conferenza "Probleme der Uebersetzung und der nachbildenden Auslegung" tenuta a Monaco il 4 giugno 1951, ed. in *Deutsche Vieteljahresschr. f. Literaturwiss. und Geistesgeschichte*, 27, 1953, 489-508. D'altro avviso Croce, vedi nota 5.

[62] Vedi *Rendiconti Istituto Lombardo*, 1941-1942, adun. 18-6-42: "per una traduzione di Hegel," estr. 3; Blass, *Handb. d. Altert. Wiss.*, I, 245 sg.

[63] Giustamente combattuta da Humboldt, *Werke*, VI, 119 e a torto difesa dal Croce, *Quaderni di Critica*, 13 (marzo 1949), 88-91.

[64] Compito, la cui proponibilita' e' negata in linea di principio dal Croce, *Estetica*, 5a ed., 76; *La poesia*, 279 sg., *Quaderni critica*, 13 (1949) 88 sg. Contro di lui Calogero, *Semantica*, 269-270. Da lui fuorviato sembra anche Wolfg. Kayser, *D. sprachiche Kunstwerk*, 298, quando asserisce addirittura "impossibili" traduzioni di poesia. Vedi in contrarion, i rilievi di Urban, *Language and reality*, 235; 738. Empirica, arbitraria a di perplessa diagnosi e' la distinzione secondo le funzioni – descrittiva o emotiva – del discorso da tradurre, che propongono Ogden & Richards, *The meaning of meaning*, 1a ed. (1923), 362-379; 8a ed. (1946), 228-241: spec. 235. Vedi intanto nostra conferenza citata ("Probleme der Uebersetzung und der nachbildenden Auslegung," 497-499.

[65] Schleiermacher, *Werke*, III, 2, 232, 239. Un procedimento di traduzione in

forma equivalente a fini normativi si ha anche nel campo del diritto internazionale privato: Vedi Balladore-Pallieri, in *Annuario del diritto comparato*, II serie, 16, 1941, 367.

[66] Riconosce giusto il ravvicinamento dell'attore al traduttore Croce, *Conversazioni critiche*, III, 71-72. Disconosce invece il ravvicinamento dell'esecutore musicale: *La Poesia*, 2a ed., 280, richiamandosi a Parente, *La musica e le arti*, 212-229.

[67] Wagner, *Hauptschr.*, 199-204; Parente, *La musica*, 136 g.

[68] Hartmann, *Problem*, 424.

[69] Baratono, *Il mio paradosso*, 24 sgg.

[70] Fabbri, *La rappresentazione moderna*, 4.

[71] Pirandello, "Illustratori, attori e traduttori," in *Nuova antologia*, 16 gennaio 1908, riedito in *Saggi*, (ed. Lo Vecchio Musti), 1939, 229-246.

[72] Pirandello, *Saggi*, cit., 231.

[73] Pirandello, *Saggi*, cit., 231.

[74] Cosi', Pirandello, *Saggi*, cit. 232.

[75] Pirandello, *Saggi*, cit. 234.

[76] Cosi', sempre, Pirandello, *Saggi*, cit. 234-235.

[77] Pirandello, *Saggi*, cit. 235.

[78] Stanislawski, *Building a character*, 1949, 20 sgg.; Wach, *Verstehen*, I, 206, n. 3; Pirandello, *Saggi*, cit., 236; cfr. 244.

[79] *Saggi*, cit., 237.

[80] *Saggi*, cit., 238, 242.

[81] Cosi', Pirandello, *Saggi*, 239.

[82] Intendiamo la meta ideale, quale viene additata ad attori e a registi da uomini di alta sensibilita' e probita', come J. Copeau e Constantino Stanislawski (*An actor prepares*, 1936; *Building a character*, 279 sgg.). Piu' avanti, (see *GTI*, § 45.b. & § 46.c.).

[83] Cosi', Pirandello, *Saggi*, 239-240.

[84] Humboldt, *Werke* (ediz. Leitsmann) VI, 179-180; 157. Cfr. Lipps, *Untersuchungen zu einer hermeneutischen Logik*, 1938, 81, 141.

[85] Questa scultoria definizione del carattere della poesia e' dovuta a Baratono, *Arte e poesia*, 1945, § 4: 48. Sulla parola interiore, Segond, *Psychologie*, § 15; 73, 80. V. Egger, *La parole Intérieure* (1881), 65 sgg, 125 sgg., e altri scritti nei prolegomeni, nota 118.

[86] In proposito, Humboldt, *Werke*, VI, 159, 174, 175, 176, 177 sg., 181; VII, 56, 57, 63; Lipps, *Unters. z. e. hermeneut. Logik*, 111; e altri scritti citati in *Categorie civilistiche interpr.* = *Hermeneutisches Manifest*, nota 17.b

[87] Giovanni Pascoli, *Pensieri e discorsi* (Zanichelli, 1907): "la mia scuola di grammatica." Vedi inoltre Ruediger, *Problema del tradurre*, 1943, 20 sgg., e altri scritti richiamati in *Categorie Civilistiche Interpr.*, alla nota 106.

[88] *Saggi*, cit., 241.

[89] Croce, *Estetica*, 5a ed., 76; *Poesia*, 2a ed., 279 sg.; *Quaderni d. critica*, n. 13 (marzo, 1949), 88 sg.; per una debole critica, Calogero, *Estetica, semantica, istorica*, 1947, 269-270; in radicale dissenso, nostra *Interpr. legge*, 180, nota 40.

[90] Su tale carattere, Baratono, *Arte e poesia*, 76, 93, 101, 176, 187, 189.

[91] Jakob Grimm, nell'epistol. con Arnim: vedi brano riferito sopra alla endnote number 20 del *GTI*, § 39.

[92] P. Abraham, in *Encyclopédie française*, XVII, 1756-II.

[93] Schleiermacher, *Werke*, III, 2 (*Methoden d. Uebersetzen*), 232, 239.

[94] Contro codesto metodo, G. Craig, *Art du Théatre*, 39 sg.; 59 sg.; C. Tamberlani, *Interpretazione nel teatro e nel cinema*, 142.

[95] Tamberlani, *L'interpretazione nel teatro e nel cinema*, 142.

[96] Parente, *La musica*, 220-224; Croce, *La poesia*, 2a ed., 282.

[97] Cfr.R. Franchini, ne *Lo Spettatore Ital.*, II, 1949, nr. 12, per il quale la traduzione *a calco* sarebbe la sola capace di non alterare la dura, ma stimolante complessita' of the Hegelian thought and of inviting to a direct trial with the original text.

[98] Da Benedetto Croce, in *Quaderni di Critica*, n. 13 (marzo 1949, 88 ssg., e da suoi seguaci, come R. Mucci in *Fiera Letteraria*, 7 agosto 194 ; *Popolo*, 5 agosto 1951 (gergo hegeliano e traduzioni a calco), o Franchini, ne *Lo Spettatore*, II, 1949, nr. 12.

[99] Cosi' Croce, in *Quaderni di Critica*, nr. 13 (1949), 89.

[100] Cfr. Giovanni Gentile, "Il diritto e il torto delle traduzioni," in *Rivista di cultura*, 1920; *Filosofia dell'arte*, p. 11, cap. I; in *Giorn. crit. fiosofia italiana*, 1950, 444-452; Vossler, *Geist u. Kultur in der Sprache*, 1925, 191; Lipps, *Unters. z. e. hermeneut. Logik*, 82 sgg.; Harbsmeier, in *Kerygma und Mythos*, I, 70; n. ril. in *Dt. Vjschr.f.Liter. wiss., 1953*, n. 18; sopra (*see GTI*, § 9).

[101] W. v. Humboldt, *Werke*, VII, 56 sgg.; M. W. Urban, *Language and Reality*, 235, 238-241.

[102] W. v. Humboldt, *Werke*, VII, 60; 64-65; cfr. *Dt. Vjschr.f.Liter. wiss.*, 1953, 493.

[103] Cosi' ancora Humboldt, *Werke*, VII, 100;; cfr. Urban, *Language and Reality*, 242; (*see GTI*, Prolegomena, note 32). Per la veduta della cibernetica, Wiener, Introd., 22.

[104] Ancora da W. v. Humboldt, *Werke*, VII, 173.

[105] E' da risalire anche qui a W. v. Humboldt, *Werke*, VI, 119.

[106] Humboldt, *Werke*, VI, 119, parla di *Allgemeingültigkeit*.

[107] Sempre da Humboldt, *Werke*, VI, 119 (see *GTI*, § 2.d, part II, nr. 10).

[108] Con Humboldt, *Werke*, VII, 176 sgg., nel cui discorso hanno rilievo particolare le espressioni "auffassende Stimmung", "Geltung" (valore espressivo) e "uberschwanken" (alludente all'eccedenza di significato).

[109] Ogden & Richards, *Meaning of meaning*, chapter II.

[110] Humboldt, *Werke*, VI, 179 sgg; H. Lipps, *Hermeneut. Logik*, 81 sg.

[111] Vedi cenni in nostra comunicazione del 18 giugno 1942, per una traduzione italiana della fenomenologia e della logica di Hegel in *Rendiconti Istituto Lombardo*, 75, 1941-42, fasc. 2; e nella conferenza "Problem d. Uebersetzung" in *Dt. Vjschr.f.Liter. wiss.*, 1953, 27, 503.

[112] Il richiamo si limita alle sole traduzioni che sono a nostra conoscenza; cfr. scr. cit. nota preced. e la traduzione di Morris, *Signs, language, and behavior*.

[113] E. De Negri, *I principii di Hegel* (Fir. N. It., 1949) introd. Formulazione del Mucci, "Gergo Hegeliano e traduzione a calco" in *Popolo*, 5 agosto 1951, in difesa del De Negri.

[114] Sul fenomeno dello "Absinken der Begriffe," Hartmann, *Probl. d. geist S.* 427-29.

[115] Sul valore in parola, Baratono, *Arte e Poesia*, 76; Porzig, *Wunder der Sprache*, 348.

[116] In proposito, Ogden & Richards, *Meaning of meaning*, 8a ed., 25-27; 1st ed., 34-37.

[117] In proposito, Morris, *Signs, language and behavior*, 1945, 347.

[118] Si rimanda alla nostra comunicazioe in *Rendiconti Istituto Lombardo*, 75, 1941-42, cit. a n. 15.

[119] Schleiermacher, *Werke*, III-II, 217; . *Dt. Vjschr.f.Liter. wiss.*, 1953, 27, 498.

[120] (See *GTI*, § 39.a & c); . *Dt. Vjschr.f.Liter. wiss.* 27, 507.

[121] Hartmann, *Probl. d. geist. S.*, cap. 52: 405-13; cap. 55: 427-34; *Festschr. Rabel*, II, 156-59; Rothacker, *Die dogmatische Denkform in then Geisteswiss.*, nella monografia dell' *Akademie der Wiss.u. der literatur*, 1954, Nr. 6, 259-264.

[122] Da Schleiermacher, "Ueber die verschiedenen Methoden des Uebersetzen" in *Vortr. b. d. Akad. d. Wiss. zu Berlin*, v. 24. Juni 1813, in *Werke*, III Abt.-II, 207-245: 218.

[123] Schleiermacher, *Werke*, III, II, 218. Cfr. Vinc. Magnoni circa i criteri adottati da Ferruccio Busoni nelle sue trascrizioni (radiotrasmiss. 25 giugno 1948).

[124] Cosi' ancora Schleiermacher, *Werke*, III, II, 219. Cfr. Hartmann, *Probl. d. geist. S.*, 185, 189, 192, 212, 217.

[125] Schleiermacher, l. cit. 220; diss. Croce, *Poesia*, 2nd ed., 103, 280.

[126] Da Schleiermacher, "Ueber die verschiedenen Methoden des Uebersetzen" in *Vortr. b. d. Akad. d. Wiss. zu Berlin*, v. 24. Juni 1813, in *Werke*, III Abt.-II, 220.

[127] Cfr, Nietzche, *Fröhl. Wiss.*, 83; *Menschliches allzumensch*, II, 126.

[128] Cfr, Goethe, "Noten u. Abhandl. zu besserem Verständnis d. westostl. Divans," in *Werke* ed. Cotta, 1885, VI 362, 641 sg. (*Dt. Vjschr.f.Liter. wiss.*, 1953, 27, 504), che distingue tre indirizzi del tradurre. Sul valore fonetico, Baratono, *Arte ePoesia*, 48-51.

[129] Schleiermacher, in *Werke*, III, II, 223; Wagner, *Hauptschriften*, 175.

[130] Cosi' sempre Schleiermacher, in *Werke*, III, II, 224; *Dt. Vjschr.f.Liter. wiss.*, 27, 503; 498, n. 30. La critica ivi rivolta a W. Kayser, *D. Sprachl. Kunstwork*, 298, calzerebbe anche contro E. Pocar, in *Dt. it. Kulturnachr*, 1953 Jul. No. nr. 31-35 vom Uebersetzen: deutsche Autoren in Italien.

[131] Cosi' sempre Schleiermacher, in *Werke*, III, II, 227; cfr. *Dt. Vjschr.f.Liter. wiss.*, 27, 505, con calzanti rifessioni (228-230) circa le condizioni propizie a questo indirizzo.

[132] Schleiermacher, in *Werke*, III, II, 231; cfr. Goethe, *Wahrheit u. Dichtung*, X, in fine; W. Friedmann, *La Traduction in Encyclopédie française*, XVII, alla voce "arti e letter. n. societa' contemporanea, sez. A (opere cn la critica; cap. III (tendenze attuali della letterat.), nr. 21, p. 1756-ii.

[133] Convinzione, sulla quale si fonda l'intera arte dell'intendere il discorse e quindi anche quella del tradurre: cfr. Schleiermacher, in *Werke*, III, II, 212, 216.
[134] Codesta meta irraggiungibile e' prospettata da Schleiermacher, in *Werke*, III, II, 232-233.
[135] Varie situazioni codeste, fatte presenti da Schleiermacher, in *Werke*, III, II, 234-237.
[136] Ritiene decisivo l'argomento Schleiermacher, in *Werke*, III, II, 238; contro la veduta del quale prendemmo posizione in *Dt. Vjschr.f.Liter. wiss.*, 27, 506 sg.
[137] In questo senso nostra conferenza "Probleme der Uebersetzung" in *Dt. Vjschr.f.Liter. wiss.*, 27, 506.
[138] In questi limiti e' fondata la critica di Schleiermacher, *loc. cit.*, 241.
[139] Espresso da Schleiermacher, in *Werke*, III, II, 239-240, nella critica che rivolge all'indirizzo in discussione. prendendo troppo alla lettera l'idea di una identificazione psicologica del traduttore con l'autore.
[140] In questo senso vedi nostra confer. citata in *Dt. Vjschr.f.Liter. wiss.*, 27, 507. Cfr. letter. cit. in *Hermeneutisches Manifest*, nota 17.b (*Festschrift f. Rabel*, II, 94).
[141] Quest'ultima obiezione e' mossa da Schleiermacher, in *Werke*, III, II, 242.
[142] Cio' nota giustamente Schleiermacher, in *Werke*, III, II, 242.
[143] Siffatta prevalenza di soggettivita' e' giustamente avvertita e messa in luce da Giovanni Gentile, *Filosofia dell'Arte*, p. II, cap. I; cfr. il buon resoconto di R. Raggiunti, "Il concetto del tradurre nel pensiero di G. Gentile," in *Giornale crit. d. filos. it.*, 1950, 449-451. Ma non e' da condividere ne' la identificazione col vero tradurre (cfr. Urban, Language, 235, 238-41) ne' la confusione tra "intendere," "rivivere," e "tradurre."
[144] Cfr. Letteratura citata nel nostro *Hermeneutisches Manifest*, alle note 20-21.a; aggiungi Rothacker, "*Die Dogmatische Denkenform in den Geisteswissenschaften*," nelle Abhandl. della *Akademie der Wissensch. u. der Lieratur*, 1954, 250-264.
[145] Tendenza codesta caratteristica della mentalita' medioevale, ma non riscontrabile in essa soltanto (Koschacher, *Europa u. d. röm. Recht*, 48 sgg, 146 seg. Qui si attinge intelligenza dei fenomeni di ricezione: sui quali vedi da ultimo Wieacker, *Privatrechtgeschichte der Neuzet*, 63-75; cfr. *Studia & doc. hist. & jur.*,1952, 292 sg.
[146] Per questi ed altri esempi si rimanda alle trattazioni di storia della giurisprudenza e del pensiero speculativo (Calasso, *Medio evo del diritto*, I, 529, 564 sg). Su di un aspetto proprio della storia della scienza, Hartmann, *Problem d. geist. Seins*, cap. 52 e 55; 408 sg., 427 sgg.
[147] Cfr. Hartmann, *Problem d. geist. Seins*, 409. Taluni, come Dessoir e Dag. Frey, *Kunstwiss. Groundfragen*, 90-91, parlano di una" Inselhaftigkeit des Kunstwerks," ma questa va intesa *cum granu salis*: vedi nostra *Hermeneut. Manifest*, nota 31 (Festschr., 106).
[148] In proposito, N. Hartmann, *Problem d. geist. Seins*, 428-430; (*see GTI*, § 35).
[149] Husserl, *Erfahrung u. Urteil*, 251 sgg, 283, 340, 377.
[150] Hartmann, *Probl. d. geist. S.*, 428 sg.
[151] Antitesi ben rilevata da N. Hartmann, *Probl. d. geist. S.*, 407-412.

[152] Cfr. tuttavia, per l'esatta comprensione del fenomeno, Berenson, *Estetica delle arti della rappresentazione visiva*, 69, 346; Focillon, *Vita delle forme*, 97-108, 139-158.

[153] Bene, N. Hartmann, *Probl. d. geist. S.*, 430 sg.; 439 sg.; cfr. 410 sg; Rothacker, *D. dogmatische Denkform*, 252-256.

[154] Si raffronti l'analogo criterio che vale in tema di trascrizione musicale. Qui, dato che ogni strumento musicale ha la sua particolare tecnica, che trascrive e traduce per strumenti diversi da quelli che aveva in vista l'opera originale, deve introdurvi gli adattamenti e le modificazioni opportune. Cosi' si regola G. S. Bach nel trascrivere il concerto in sol magg. e altre composizioni di Vivaldi.

[155] Droysen, *Historik*, 115 sgg.; Freyer, *Theorie des objektiven Geistes*, 3a ed. 1934, 78, 105-9: (*see GTI*, § 20.b). Con particolare riguardo alle interpolazioni introdotte nei testi del diritto romano, F. Schulz, *Einführung in das Studium der Digesten*, 1916, 19 sgg, 36 sgg., 41sgg.; Bonfante, *Storia del Diritto Romano*, 3a ed., II, 126-171; e la bibliografia ivi richiamata a p. 127. Fra i contributi posteriori vanno segnalati: Prinsheim, "Die Entstehung des Digestenplanes u, die Rechtsschulen," in *Atti Congresso Internazionale*, 1933, I, 449; e contributi in *Studi Bonfante*, I, 551; Scherillo, *Manuale di storia* (1950), 507-521.

[156] Bonfante, *Storia*, II, 168; Scherillo, *Manuale di storia* (1950), 518.

[157] Grosso, "La tecnica interpolazionistica e il codice civile" in *Stato e Diritto*, 1942, nr. 6 (nov. dic.).

[158] Cfr. R. Feenstra, *Interpretatio multiplex; een beschowing over ten agn. Crisis van het Romeinse Recht*, 1953, 21 (rec. Kaser, *Zschr. d. sav. St.*, 71, 1954, 546).

[159] In proposito, G.G. Archi, "La Valutazione Critica del Corpus Juris : considerazioni di un Romanista su problemi di diritto bizantino," in *Atti VIII Congesso Studi Bizantini*, II, 277-290.

[160] Da H. J. Wolff, *Historical Introduction*, 140; da Fr. Schulz, da Fr. Wiacker, *Sav. Zschr.*, 1942.

[161] Cfr. L. Mitteis, *Reichsrecht u. Volksrecht in den Ostl. Provinzen d. rom. Kaiserreichs*, 1891, 209 sgg.; Pringsheim, in *The Journal of Juristic Papyrology*, 1953-1954, 163-168.

[162] Questo fenomeno e' messo bene in rilievo con talune eloquenti esemplificazioni dell'Archi, in "La Valutazione Critica del Corpus Juris : considerazioni di un Romanista su problemi di diritto bizantino," in *Atti VIII Congesso Studi Bizantini*, II, 280-287. (*see GTI*, Prolegomena, § 7-8).

[163] Non erano mancati altri tentativi di rielaborazione e compilazione: vedi in Arangio-Ruiz, "Precedenti scolastici del Digesto," in *Conferenze per il XIV centenario delle Pandette*, 1931, 287-319; "Di alcune fonti post-classiche del Digesto": memoria letta all'accademia delle scienze di Napoli (Atti, 54, 1931, parte I).

[164] F. Schulz, *Einführung in das Studium der Digesten*, 38 sg. Per S. Solazzi, *Glossemi in Gaio*, l'ipotesi di glossemi assume proporzioni esorbitanti sotto l'influenza di un pregiudizio di "kyriolexia" (Schleiermacher, *Hermeneutik*, 131, 134) che sta in palese contrasti con canoni ermeneutici.

[165] In proposito, Wieacker, "Ratio scripta: das röm. Recht u. die abendlandische Rechtswiss." in *Vom rom. Recht*, 1944, 195-284; ancora Feenstra, *Interpretation multiplex*, 20-26.

[166] Bene, G.G. Archi, "La Valutazione Critica del Corpus Juris : considerazioni di un Romanista su problemi di diritto bizantino," in *Atti VIII Congesso Studi Bizantini*, II, 284-290; letteratura ivi 279, 283; anche in *Rivista Italiana Scienze Giuristiche*, 1951, 220.

[167] Riferiamo ancora la caratterizzazione della poesia formulata da Baratono in *Arte e Poesia*, § 4, pagina 48.

[168] Cfr. W. Kayser, *Das sprachliche Kunstwerk*, 1948, 298, 299.

[169] Wilamowitz-Möllendorf, "Was ist Uebersetzen?" (Vorrede zum Hippolitos), in *Reden u. Vorträge*, 3rd ed., 129; Pascoli, *Pensieri e discorsi* (Zanichelli, 1907: "la mia scuola di grammatica." (*see GTI*, § 39.c).

[170] Tale e' la veduta di Benedetto Croce, *Estetica*, 5a ed., 76; *La poesia*, 2a ed., 279 sgg., che trova pur sempre volenterosi seguaci in chi preferisce adagiarsi sull'autorita' del suo verbo, senza rimeditare il problema: cfr.R. Franchini, in *Lo spettatore italiano*, II, 1949, nr 12 (dicembre); Erw. Pocar, *Vom Uebertsetzen in Deutsch-ital Kulturnachrichten*, 31-35 (1953); nostra critica in *Dt. Vjschr.f.Liter. wiss.*, 27, 1953, 498 sgg.

[171] Cosi' ancora in adesione pedissequa alla veduta del Croce, R. Mucci, "Gergo hegeliano e traduzioni a calco," in *Fiera Litteraria*, IV, 32: 7 agosto 1949 e nel giornale *Il Popolo di Roma* del 5 agosto 1951. Mediocre la traduzione tentata dall'Ungaretti delle liriche di William Blake e di St. Mallarmé: in essa appare accresciuta una irremediabile carenza dell'originale. Meritano le piu' ampie riserve le versioni dall'inglese (Shakespeare) tentate dal Montale, e quindi dal greco (Sofocle) intraprese dal Quasimodo.

[172] Per una critica del rigorismo, N. Harftmann, *Ethik*, 233 sgg, 240sg, 348 sg. §§

[173] Vedi inoltre nostra conferenza, "Probleme der Uebersetzung u. d. nachbild. Ausleg.," 499, 503-505.

[174] Istruttiva e' anche una preziosa confessione di Maurice Clavel ha reso nel presentare al pubblico parigino, il 27 novembre 1954, il dramma *Irene Innocente* (che egli ama qualificare *Irene sauvée*).

C'est surtout par L'Ile aux Chèvres que le public parisien connait Ugo Betti. Mais l'oeuvre, si elle donne une idée exacte du talent de l'auteur, nous cache l'homme. Angelo le baladin est un préchrétien, un faune, un Scythe, un Etrusque; et si le christianisme s'exprime dans la pièce par le personage d'Agata et le dénoument, ce n'est pas le christianisme de Betti. Tout au plus la première moitié ....

Dieu, dans L'Ile aux Chèvres, n'est que justice et nécéssité. La damnation est irrémissible. Une pensée formulée, une goutte d'eau tombée le sont pour toujours. Il y a même, plus q'une résignation, une joie sombre, une tranquillité du damné. Or le Dieu de Betti, celui d'Irène, du Jouer, de Pas d'Amour, de l'ensemble de son oeuvre est, par delà ses lois, une fois tout bien pesé, grâce, miséricorde, charité, arbitraire. L'orgueil, l'endurcissement, la révolte sont encore une manière de lui parler. Betti me confiait que s'il avait à traiter Don Juan, il nous l'aurait donné sauvé sans repentir. "Le mal est une prière." Peut-

être eût-il sauvé Satan, comme Papini. Il lui sera d'autant plus facile de sauver la petite Irène. Il n'y aura pas même besoin de conversion, de miracle; le ciel n'a pas à faire un coup d'éclat. Un très vague reflet de lumière d'aprés l'orage a transfiguré la flaque sur le chemin. Elle avait donc toujours été transparente. Un chrétien se dira, au denouement d'Irène, que Dieu n'a pas parlé, que nul n'a parlè à Dieu, mais que la Vierge Marie s'est chargée, silencieusement, de toute l'affaire.

Ou encore je pense a ce passage d'Elie, ou le prophète, cherchant entre les vents et les tempêtes de l terre quel est le souffle divin, le reconnait enfin dan un petite brise. Elle murmure au long d'Irène Innocente. Elle entrouve la porte et prend l'âme au passage. Et ce n'est point un symbole. Tout était grâce et nous n'aurons eu que de la nature. Tout était rêve poètique, petite légende de rédemption, et nous auront pourtant assisté à une histoire, une action, que dis-je, une intrigue des plus réelles. Je crois même qu'Irène est ce qu'on appelle "une bonne pièce."

Je la connait depuis des années. J'En ai fait trois adaptations successives: aucune ne me satisfait. A chaque fois que je retravaille, mon metier ne me sert de rien. Je précise et le charme s'en va. Je veux garder le rêve et soudain j'en fabrique. Une loi absolute s'impose: pas un "morceau" de poésie, pas un "effet" de théâtre. Traduction littérale? Absurde, puisqu'il faut, au delà du métier et de l'art, rendre l'hésitation tremblante, la maladresse de la grâce: on n'obtiendrait qu'une traduction maladroite. Une seule solution: lire, relire, relire encore, essayer d'etre l'auteur, ecrire! ainsi on obtient souvent des effets étonnant de fidelité. Mais je ne vois pas comment j'aurais pu tenter de le faire si je n'avais pas connu longuement Ugo Betti. Et j'aurais bien aimé lui soumettre cette troisième hésitante d'Irène Innocente, afin qu'il puisse encore, d'un mot, par-ci par-là, corriger un excès de travail, une habilité inutile.

Mais les sproblems que je pose––va-t-on me dire––ne sont-ils pas les mêmes pour toute adaptation? Peut-être, mais alors je dois avouer que dans mes adaptations précédentes, j'ai été prodigieux d'aplomb et d'inconscience, puisque voici la première qui me fait peur, sur la quelle je ne puis me prononcer, en bien ou en mal, ni même croire l'avis, bon ou mauvais, de personne. Je suis depuis quatre ans devant d'Irène Innocente comme un petit docteur d'Eglise devant les Fioretti. Je me récuse. Et si Paris demain n'est pas bouleversé, je m'accuse.

Printed in Great Britain
by Amazon